VICTORIAN MANSION FLOWER SHOP MYSTERIES

Woes By Any Other Name

Jan Fields

AnniesFiction.com

Books in the Victorian Mansion Flower Shop Mysteries series

A Fatal Arrangement
Bloomed to Die
The Mistletoe Murder
My Dearly Depotted
Digging Up Secrets
Planted Evidence
Loot of All Evil
Pine and Punishment
Herbal Malady
Deadhead and Buried
The Lily Vanishes
A Cultivated Crime
Suspicious Plots
Weeds of Doubt
Thorn to Secrecy
A Seedy Development
Woes By Any Other Name
Noel Way Out
Rooted in Malice
Absent Without Leaf

. . . and more to come!

Woes By Any Other Name
Copyright © 2019 Annie's.

All rights reserved. No part of this publication may be reproduced, stored in a retrieval system, or transmitted in any form or by any means—electronic, mechanical, photocopying, recording or otherwise—without the prior written permission of the publisher. The only exception is brief quotations in printed reviews. For information address Annie's, 306 East Parr Road, Berne, Indiana 46711-1138.

The characters and events in this book are fictional, and any resemblance to actual persons or events is coincidental.

Library of Congress-in-Publication Data
Woes By Any Other Name / by Jan Fields
p. cm.
I. Title
2018968054

AnniesFiction.com
(800) 282-6643
Victorian Mansion Flower Shop Mysteries™
Series Creators: Shari Lohner, Janice Tate
Editor: Elizabeth Morrissey
Cover Illustrator: Bob Kayganich

10 11 12 13 14 | Printed in China | 9 8 7 6 5 4 3 2 1

1

A chilly breeze slipped up the street and ruffled Kaylee Bleu's long, dark hair despite the knit hat she'd put on before leaving The Flower Patch. Shivering slightly, she wondered if she needed to stretch her legs as much as she'd thought when she'd left her shop.

She glanced down at her dog, Bear, to see if he was feeling the effects of the crisp autumn day in Turtle Cove, Washington. If the little dachshund was cold, he didn't show it. He held his head high and pranced, or got as close to prancing as he could with his short legs. The sight put a smile on Kaylee's lips despite the chill. "You're looking dapper," she told him.

Bear peered up at her quizzically, showing off the bow tie Kaylee had chosen for the day. She thought the pattern of fall leaves was particularly appropriate for November, and Bear was handsome as always. As if he could read her mind, the dog wagged his tail and offered her a single friendly bark though he never broke his stride, trotting along the sidewalk with purpose. Bear took his walks seriously and wasn't prone to dawdling, especially not when they were walking toward the ferry launch. The little dog loved the ferry. Kaylee didn't know if it was the wealth of interesting scents coming off Puget Sound or the chance for so many new arrivals to admire him. She rather suspected it was a bit of both.

Not that Kaylee disagreed with him. The bustle of people streaming off the ferry to visit Orcas Island never ceased to fascinate her. She also loved walking along the shoreline and watching the bald eagles soar and dip as they fished for breakfast.

She even enjoyed the slightly fishy salt spray. She thought of those moments as her reminders of how blessed she was to live in such an incredibly beautiful place.

Kaylee's wandering thoughts were brought sharply into focus as Bear suddenly lunged forward, his front legs nearly lifting off the ground in his eagerness to rush ahead. "What's your hurry?" she asked him as she examined the sidewalk ahead, expecting to see one of her friends coming their way.

About a half a block away, she spotted a couple peering into the front window of Glasstastic, one of the trendy new businesses that sometimes popped up unexpectedly on the island. This one was an art gallery and gift shop that, as its name implied, specialized in glass merchandise. Kaylee thought the works inside were lovely but considerably out of her price range for something that would sit on a shelf, inviting dust.

Kaylee noticed the couple for two reasons. For one, they were an extremely attractive pair, as if they'd stepped off a screen where they portrayed the perfect young lovers. The slender woman, with coal-black hair that hung as long and straight as Kaylee's, pointed at the window and tilted her face up toward her companion, her teeth flashing brilliantly white. The man beside her was only slightly taller, but he had broad shoulders and a head of close-cropped red curls. His teeth remained hidden behind a tight smile, and he seemed mildly annoyed by whatever the woman was saying.

The other reason Kaylee noticed the couple—and surely the reason for Bear's excitement—was that each of them held a leash in one hand, and on the end of each leash was a dachshund. Kaylee was struck by how much the two dogs resembled Bear. If he hadn't been wearing his bow tie, it might have been hard to tell him apart from them. They were the same rich russet color—and their enthusiasm ramped up to match Bear's as they noticed a fellow dachshund approaching.

When Kaylee drew closer to the couple, the man's rich baritone rolled toward her clearly. "With as much as we travel, buying something so fragile isn't wise," he said. "It'll become the world's most dangerous jigsaw puzzle the first time the dogs run into whatever table you put it on."

"Don't be such a grouch," the woman replied, her voice musical and equally carrying. "We're done traveling, and I can finally have exactly the home of my dreams."

"Another sculpture is an expense we don't need, Belinda."

She poked him lightly. "You let me worry about that."

The man grunted in disagreement, and it appeared he was going to argue further, but Belinda had caught sight of Bear. She squealed and rushed toward Kaylee, but stopped several feet away. "What a handsome boy! Will he mind if we come say hi? Sullivan is very friendly."

"I think he'll have a nervous breakdown if you don't," Kaylee said with a laugh while her dog nearly danced with excitement. "Bear adores making new friends."

"Wonderful." The woman hurried closer. The two dachshunds sniffed each other, their tails whipping happily back and forth. Kaylee heard a yip from the third dachshund, who was straining at the end of his leash. The man holding the lead observed the women with a scowl.

Belinda waved her companion forward. "Rhett, bring Gilbert over. Don't be a grump."

The man sighed deeply and walked over. Soon all three dogs were happily getting acquainted while the women beamed at them. Belinda thrust out her right hand toward Kaylee. "I'm Belinda Case. This is my husband, Rhett. Do you live here on Orcas Island? It's so beautiful."

"I do live here. I'm Kaylee Bleu. It's lovely to meet you." She shook Belinda's hand, then gestured up the street. "I own the flower shop a few blocks that way. Are you staying in Turtle Cove?"

Belinda's expression brightened still more. "We just moved here," she said, almost breathless, as if the thrill of being there was almost overwhelming. "Our little house even has a name—Robin's Nest. Don't you just love that?"

"How charming! My house is called Wildflower Cottage," Kaylee said. "I love the naming of houses. They become such a big part of our lives. Why shouldn't they have their own names?"

Belinda beamed. "I feel the same way."

"It's silly," Rhett grumbled. "I'm going to call it 'the house.'"

"Party pooper," Belinda said, wrinkling her nose at her husband. He only crossed his arms over his chest and frowned in mild disapproval. She ignored him and smiled at Kaylee. "Did you say your little guy's name is Bear? I love that, and the bow tie is brilliant. I should get some for Gilbert and Sullivan."

Kaylee laughed aloud in surprise as the names registered with her. "Gilbert and Sullivan? You must love musicals."

"I do," Belinda agreed. "And it suits them. They're both little hams, which is good since they've been in a lot of plays."

"Dog actors? That must be interesting." Kaylee wondered what being a dog's stage mom entailed. "And also a lot of work."

Gilbert and Sullivan had nearly tied themselves together as they danced around Bear, and Belinda untangled the leashes with the ease of frequent practice. "Not so much for us since we're usually on the stage with them. Rhett and I are actors too, and Rhett is also a writer and director." She patted his arm with her free hand. "He's the whole package."

The praise elicited a grudging smile from him.

"I can't imagine acting," Kaylee said. "I think I would collapse from sheer embarrassment."

"I thrive on it," Belinda said. Then she cocked her head and examined Kaylee appraisingly. "It's too bad you don't want to try acting. You have a great look. I'd love to have you in the play we're casting here."

"A play?" Kaylee raised her eyebrows in surprise. "On the island?"

Belinda bounced lightly on her toes with excitement. "Yes, it's going to be a whirlwind to get it ready by the end of November, but it's a short piece. I think of it as a test drive of our new theater. We bought the old ropewalk on the waterfront and restored it." Her expression grew concerned. "I hope you're not one of those people who think old buildings should never be repurposed."

Kaylee shrugged. "It's far better than letting them decay until they fall down. I suppose it depends on whether it's a respectful restoration."

"We've definitely tried," Belinda said.

"Sparing no cost, for whatever good it will do," Rhett grumbled. "$5,000 seemed pretty ridiculous for new front doors."

Belinda made a playful shooing motion at her husband. "It's worth every penny, dear." She returned her attention to Kaylee. "We used locals in the restoration as much as possible."

"That's always appreciated," Kaylee said. "I think it's great that it's going to be a theater." She also thought it was a brave idea. She was vaguely aware of hearing about work on the ropewalk and knew the old factory wasn't exactly in one of the touristy neighborhoods. "Just so you know, though, we're heading into our off-season. The crowds have thinned down substantially already, and once winter hits, Orcas Island becomes a string of small, very quiet towns. I hope you're not counting on a lot of tourists if your play premieres at the end of November."

"That doesn't worry me," Belinda replied. "As I said, this is more of a test run of the renovation. That way, we'll be totally ready in the spring when the crowds pick up again. The play we're doing is going to be fun. It's a romantic romp, a comedy of errors. Rhett wrote it, and it's so funny."

Kaylee snuck a quick glance at the silent, brooding man and couldn't quite picture him as the author of such a piece. *There must be hidden depths to him.* "Sounds fun. I'll be there on opening night if I can."

"Tell your friends." Belinda bent down and scooped up Sullivan. The little dog wriggled in her arms for a moment before settling down. "We're holding open auditions starting Friday. We have a troupe that we've brought with us from the mainland, but I want to build connections to thespians in the community as well. You should come try out."

Kaylee took a small step back, aghast at the idea of acting in a stage play. "I don't think I'm cut out for acting."

"Even if you're not, it'll give you a chance to cheer on your neighbors." She squeezed the bicep of the man beside her. "Auditions are always a good time, aren't they, Rhett?"

"They do tend to be unusual," Rhett said.

"Perhaps I'll come then, though you definitely won't see me on the stage." Kaylee glanced down as she felt a tug on her pants. She saw that Bear had run around one of her legs, wrapping the leash with him. Kaylee bent to untangle him, then lifted him, leaving Gilbert panting up at Bear, tail still wagging.

"You know, it's amazing how much your Bear resembles Gilbert and Sullivan." Belinda reached out to rub the top of Bear's head. "We actually bought these guys *because* they were identical. It lets us use whichever dog is in the mood for acting. But the play Rhett wrote this time uses both dogs, so we don't have an understudy. Do you think Bear would enjoy that?"

Kaylee considered. "I think he'd love it, but I'm not sure if he's properly trained for it. He knows sit and stay, but he doesn't have many other tricks in his repertoire. Not many that he didn't think up on his own, anyway."

"That's not a problem," Belinda said. "They won't be doing anything unusual. And they're on a leash the whole time. One of the key plot points has to do with the main characters accidentally swapping dogs, and then the confusion that ensues. Bear would need to come to rehearsals, but they wouldn't be overly demanding."

"I promise to consider it," Kaylee said.

"Wonderful." Belinda beamed as brightly as if Kaylee had fully committed instead of giving a vague maybe. "I'll see you there." She turned to Rhett. "We need to get going. Everyone is waiting for us at the theater."

Rhett rolled his eyes. "Because I was the one holding us up."

Belinda linked her arm through his. "Don't be such a bear." Then she giggled and nodded toward Kaylee. "We have a Bear now, so you can give up the role."

With a last warm goodbye, Belinda walked off with her husband. Kaylee watched them go. She definitely suspected Belinda Case would leave a mark on Turtle Cove.

Having spent so much time chatting with the actors, Kaylee decided against walking the rest of the way to the ferry. She didn't want to stretch her break out quite so long. Though Mary Bishop, her assistant at the flower shop, never complained about being left alone, Kaylee tried not to abuse Mary's kind heart and good humor. Besides, Kaylee was chilled clear through.

"We'd better get inside again where it's warm," she told Bear and set him on the sidewalk. She was glad when he let her tug him toward the shop without resisting. Sometimes sudden changes to their walking plan weren't always met with flexibility. The little dog didn't like missing out on meeting new people at the ferry, but apparently Gilbert and Sullivan had temporarily satisfied his craving for new friends.

The Flower Patch only had two customers when Kaylee

walked in, and they were quietly browsing in different parts of the shop. It was clear evidence of the change of seasons. The flower shop bustled throughout the spring and summer, grew quiet between Halloween and Thanksgiving, then ramped up again for Christmas.

"Sorry to be gone so long," Kaylee said to Mary as she unclipped the leash from Bear's collar. He shook himself, though Kaylee couldn't imagine what he was shaking off.

Mary stood behind the counter with her hands wrapped around a mug, and Bear pranced over to where she stood. "Don't worry about it," Mary said. "It's been quiet. I hope you two didn't freeze out there. I think winter is trying to elbow autumn out of the way early this year."

"It is a little chilly," Kaylee admitted. "But we had a great walk. We met some new residents."

Mary raised both eyebrows. "New residents of Turtle Cove?"

"Apparently," Kaylee said. "Belinda and Rhett Case. They bought a cottage called Robin's Nest."

"Oh, I know that one," Mary said. "It's on Greenman Street. It's adorable, though it doesn't have much space for gardening."

Kaylee almost smiled at the reproof in Mary's voice. Like Kaylee and their two close friends, DeeDee Wilcox and Jessica Roberts, Mary was a member of the Petal Pushers, a local gardening club. They didn't quite *live* for their gardens, but they did love them dearly.

"I think Belinda and Rhett may be a little too busy for gardening anyway," Kaylee said. "Belinda told me they bought the old ropewalk and are converting it into a theater."

"I saw that someone was working on that building." Mary set her mug down on the counter. "I'm glad. It's quite historic, from a time when people had to make rope in long buildings so they could twist the fibers that stretched the length of the building."

"You're sure up on your town history, aren't you?"

Mary smiled. "I saw a fascinating presentation by the historical society about it once. Apparently the ropewalk couldn't make a rope any longer than the building itself. That's why the factories were so long. The ropewalk here was once over a thousand feet long, but part of the building was taken down years ago when the factory first closed."

"That is interesting." Kaylee leaned on her elbows on the counter. "It'll be fun to have a theater group in Turtle Cove, though they're picking an odd time to begin. Belinda said they'd be opening auditions to the community soon. Their first show is a romantic comedy."

"Won't that be fun?" Mary asked, her eyes sparkling at the idea.

"I hope so, since they asked me to consider letting Bear be in the play."

Again Mary's eyebrows went up. "The play needs a dachshund?"

"More than one, actually." Kaylee told Mary about Gilbert and Sullivan, describing the two friendly little dachshunds and how much Bear had enjoyed them. "It was the most amazing thing. Gilbert and Sullivan look enough like Bear that it's hard to believe they aren't all from the same litter. And they're both so sweet. Belinda said they usually only have one dog role, and the two dogs share it. When one gets tired or stubborn, the other takes over. But this time, the play has two roles for dachshunds, so they need an understudy."

Realization bloomed on Mary's face. "Bear would be perfect. Are you going to do it?"

Kaylee sighed. "I'm not sure. I think Bear would love it. He has relished every chance he's ever gotten to take part in community events." She giggled. "Remember when DeeDee's girls dressed him up as a hot dog for the pet parade? There aren't that many dogs who would have hammed it up quite so enthusiastically."

"Bear's not a ham," Mary said loyally. "He's civic-minded." As if to assuage possible hurt feelings in the little dog, she followed up her remark by bending down to scratch him behind the ears.

"Bear may love the limelight, but I'm not sure I share his sentiments. I don't know how much time we're talking about for him to play understudy. Belinda insisted it wouldn't be arduous, but she also said he'd have to be at rehearsals."

"You shouldn't bother. It'll be a waste of your time."

Kaylee spun sharply to see that one of the women browsing in the shop had approached the counter. The woman was short and stout with a head of wild blonde curls and brown eyes that squinted in Kaylee's direction.

Kaylee blinked a few times. "I beg your pardon?"

"The play. You shouldn't bother going out for auditions," the woman replied. "It's a disaster waiting to happen. And it probably will never open."

"And what makes you say that?" Mary asked.

The woman looked at her slyly. "I'd rather keep my reasons to myself. But mark my words, that play is doomed."

Before Kaylee could come up with a response to the startling comments, the woman marched out of the shop. As the door swung closed behind her, Kaylee wondered exactly what secrets she had been hinting at. With a shiver, Kaylee scooped up Bear and gave him a worried hug.

The woman's warning had felt a little too real.

2

Throughout the week, Kaylee vacillated about the play. One moment, she was sure she would take Bear and let him audition. The next, she decided she wouldn't audition, but she'd go in order to show her support for the new venture. Still later, she thought maybe she'd stay home and have a cozy evening with Bear. It was as if the options were balls bouncing around in her head, and she didn't reach out to catch one until the light began to fade on Friday evening.

Pulling her red Ford Escape into the theater's newly paved parking lot, Kaylee still wasn't sure if she'd made the right choice in coming. "We could go home," she said to Bear, but his excited yip told her that he was eager for an adventure. "Fine. We'll go in."

Once the decision was made, Kaylee hopped out of the car quickly, as if to keep herself from changing her mind. She knew she was being silly. Letting Bear be in the play wouldn't be a big deal. He'd have fun and charm everyone he met—she didn't doubt that. When she took a moment to think about it, she knew that the real reason she shied away from the idea was her own feelings about public performances.

As a former plant taxonomy professor at the University of Washington, she had plenty of experience with public speaking. She had stood in front of a classroom full of reluctant students many times. But somehow, the thought of talking about her passion for plants was a very different thing from performing on a stage. Though he was perfectly capable of jumping down from the back seat by himself, she picked up Bear and cuddled him. "I think I'm getting stage fright for you."

Bear gave her a reassuring doggie kiss on the chin.

"You're right," she agreed. "We're a team, and we'll be fine."

Kaylee stood holding Bear for a moment as she looked toward the old building. The battered bricks were weathered but seemed in good shape. As Mary had said, the old factory was basically a long box and now bore an oversize black awning and a large wooden sign identifying it as the *Ropeworks Playhouse*. Though the overall theme was rustic, the lighting in the parking lot and the front of the theater was modern enough that it was easy to see the lot filling up. *I guess I'm the only one with stage fright.*

With so many cars pulling in, Kaylee decided to carry Bear into the theater for safety. Once inside, she snapped on his leash and put him down. Bear immediately began sniffing the old wooden floors, as well as everything else he could reach. In the lobby, a sign on an easel directed all those auditioning to sign in at the folding table against one wall and then wait in the theater until their names were called. Kaylee wasn't sure if Bear needed to sign in, but just in case, she headed for the crowd around the table.

Near the table, Kaylee recognized a blonde head at the edge of the group. "DeeDee!"

DeeDee Wilcox waved back. Almost immediately, DeeDee's younger daughter, Polly, leaned out from behind her mother and squealed. "Bear!" The girl rushed over to squat and pat Bear on the head.

"Polly," her mother called after her. "You need to stay with me."

Polly popped to her feet and tugged on Kaylee's free hand. "Come on," she said. "You can stand with us."

"I don't want to cut in line," Kaylee said as the little girl towed her toward DeeDee.

"It's not exactly a line," DeeDee said as she put a protective arm around Polly's shoulders. "I think we're more of an amorphous clump."

"Amorphous?" Kaylee asked.

DeeDee grinned. "It's Zoe's word of the day."

Zoe, who was quickly approaching her teen years, stood next to her mother, watching her sister with irritation until she heard her name. Her attention snapped to Kaylee and she said, "Amorphous is an adjective that describes something without a clearly defined form or shape. Are you going to be in the play?"

"I am," Polly sang out before Kaylee could speak.

"Maybe," DeeDee told her daughter, her voice full of motherly caution. "There's no guarantee that either of you will get a part, so you need to be prepared for that. Let's audition first. Just go out there and do your best."

"Right." Polly's head bobbed in agreement. Then she whispered to Kaylee, "I'm going to be in the play."

Kaylee laughed. "You probably will." She couldn't imagine DeeDee's daughters failing at anything they put their minds to.

Zoe gave her sister another glare, then spoke to Kaylee in a precocious tone. "Are you auditioning?"

"Not me," Kaylee said. "Bear is auditioning to be an understudy for the dachshunds who are in the play."

Polly's eyes widened. "There are dogs in the play? This is going to be so much fun!" She clapped her hands and jumped in place.

"Next!" The voice announced, and the crowd mashed a little closer to the table. Polly whirled at the sound and squeezed between a stout couple to get a better spot.

"Polly!" DeeDee called, then sighed and addressed her eldest. "Can you get your sister, please?"

Zoe echoed her mother's sigh before vanishing into the crowd.

"I hope I don't regret the decision to let them audition," DeeDee said to Kaylee.

"I'm sure they'll have fun. The couple running the show seems to know what they're doing. I met them the other day when I was walking Bear." Kaylee remembered the encounter with the unpleasant stranger at her shop. "Though it's possible it won't really matter. Maybe."

"What do you mean?" DeeDee's attention laser focused on Kaylee. As the owner of a mystery bookshop, DeeDee loved a good plot twist, but she found real life mysteries a bit alarming if they might involve her daughters.

"Nothing probably," Kaylee said, already regretting her comment. "We had someone in the shop the other day who overheard Mary and me talking about the play. The woman said she thought the production was doomed. I suppose she may have been talking about the money involved. When I met them, one of the owners seemed to think they weren't spending their renovation funds wisely." Kaylee waved a hand to reference the beautiful workmanship shown in the lobby. The style was rustic but modern in feel, and Kaylee knew it had to be a huge change from what had once been a long, mostly open building. "This must have been a pricey project."

"No doubt," DeeDee said. "My husband told me he'd been inside this building before and though it appeared structurally sound, it had significant signs of disrepair from being unused for so long. They must have had to fix a lot of those issues before they even got to the aesthetic stuff." Her gaze darted toward the dense crowd where Polly and Zoe had disappeared. "So you don't think the woman was hinting at anything ominous?"

"I'm sure she wasn't," Kaylee said, hoping her tone didn't sound as doubtful as she felt.

Zoe popped out of the crowd, hauling Polly by the hand. "She'd already gotten to the table and signed up, so I went ahead and signed up too."

"Well, I should scold you," DeeDee said with a frown. "But I'll be glad to get out of this crowd." She offered an apologetic smile to Kaylee. "Do you mind if we abandon you and go get seats? We can save you one."

"That would be great, thanks," Kaylee said.

DeeDee and the girls eased out of the crowd, and Kaylee braced herself for the wait. For a moment, she wished Polly had signed Bear up too. *No, I shouldn't benefit from Polly's naughtiness.*

To Kaylee's relief, Bear waited patiently beside her as if he stood in line all the time. Behind the table, a young woman responded with boundless patience as each person signed in and asked questions. When Kaylee approached, she noticed the young woman's eyes were slightly red, as if she might have been crying earlier, though she seemed to perk up when she saw Bear. "Auntie Belinda was right," she said. "He could be Gilbert and Sullivan's long-lost brother. Is it okay if I pet him?"

"Sure," Kaylee said. "Bear loves attention."

The girl's sweet smile spread into a grin. "Bear? I love that name." She rubbed his ears. "Aren't you handsome? Auntie Belinda already signed him up, so I'll make a note that he arrived and you two can go into the theater. I think they're about ready to start."

"Thanks."

Entering the auditorium through worn wooden doors with thick iron handles, Kaylee found the rustic theme continued into the theater, where rough-hewn beams and dark walls set a cozy, woodsy tone. Granted, however rustic the decor was, she could tell the lights and rigging above the stage were clearly brand-new and state-of-the-art. *Whoever's paying the bills for this project has put in a lot of money.*

Kaylee slipped into the open chair beside DeeDee and her daughters. She settled Bear into her lap just as Belinda Case appeared on the stage, front and center. The young woman was elegant and beautiful in a blue floral dress, with her hair skillfully twisted into an updo. She carried a long-stemmed lily in one hand. Though she couldn't clearly see it, Kaylee recognized it immediately as a *Lilium auratum* and wondered where Belinda had gotten it. Kaylee didn't have any at her shop. The large lilies were grown primarily in Japan, and it was costly to have flowers flown in from so far away unless they were for a special order.

Her preoccupation with the lily nearly made Kaylee miss the first words of Belinda's opening speech, in which she welcomed everyone to the Ropeworks Playhouse and expressed her excitement to be part of their wonderful community.

Kaylee was struck again by how lovely the young woman was, especially since she radiated joy and friendliness.

The actress continued with her opening. "With our commitment to community involvement, we knew we wanted to use some local actors in our first production. But first, let me introduce you to the family we brought with us—the Victory Players!" Belinda began to clap as a small group of people walked onstage.

Kaylee spotted the young girl who had signed everyone in, then she recognized someone who surprised her even more. The stout, curly-haired woman who had made the dire prediction about the failure of the first show was a member of the troupe. Kaylee scooted slightly forward in her seat as Belinda introduced each person, eager to hear the name of the mystery woman.

"And this is Delia Putnam," Belinda said finally, sweeping her arm toward the older woman. "Delia has appeared in a number of comedies in playhouses throughout the Pacific Northwest. Her most recent role was Miss Hannigan in *Annie*, for which she received stellar reviews. We're grateful to have her and her talents in our troupe."

Kaylee watched the woman bow slightly to the audience, beaming at everyone like someone's kindly grandmother. It was hard to believe she had been all gloom and doom only a few days before at The Flower Patch. The fact that she was a member of the troupe made Kaylee nervous. *Why would someone so connected with the show be going around telling people that it's doomed?*

When she had finished introductions, Belinda focused her attention on the crowd again. "Who knows which of you will be joining our troupe for this first performance, and perhaps for many to come in the future?"

She went on to describe the roles they would be filling, mainly small parts playing townspeople. Kaylee was glad to hear there were several roles for children since it would mean DeeDee's girls were likely to get cast. *Of course, if the show isn't going to work out, maybe that's setting them up for disappointment.*

Bear must have sensed Kaylee's disquiet because he shifted in her lap to nuzzle her hand. "It's okay," she whispered. "I'm being silly."

"Silly about what?" DeeDee asked quietly.

Kaylee gestured toward the stage. "The older woman, Delia, is the one who I told you about, the lady at the shop who didn't think the show was worth auditioning for."

"That's odd."

"I had the same reaction."

DeeDee frowned. "There's no way I'm going to get the girls out of here without auditioning. So I guess I'll have to hope for the best."

The auditions were handled efficiently and kindly, with everyone given the time they needed to make the best possible impression. As she watched, Kaylee thought there was certainly no reason to doubt the quality of the show—or the courage of her neighbors. She couldn't imagine trying to recite a monologue as half the town watched, and she could see more than one person openly sweating with nerves as they climbed the stairs to the stage. Kaylee was impressed with how compassionately Belinda handled each one. Within moments, Belinda could calm even the most fearful performer.

Kaylee most enjoyed all the children's auditions, especially DeeDee's girls, who clearly threw themselves into each thing they were asked to do. In Kaylee's biased opinion, Zoe and Polly were brilliant.

After the children, Belinda called Kaylee and Bear up to the stage. DeeDee squeezed Kaylee's arm as she stood up. "You two will be great," she whispered.

Kaylee hoped so. Though she had slowly relaxed while watching and getting caught up in the audition performances, all that had been undone the second Bear's name was called. Kaylee felt nearly sick with nerves. Bear took it all in stride, gazing eagerly around as Kaylee carried him up to the stage.

Much to Kaylee's surprise, Belinda gave her a quick hug. "Thanks for coming. I know this can be scary, but you'll be fine, and Bear will be great."

"I believe the last part at least," Kaylee said, trying for a light tone, but recognizing that she sounded as scared as she felt.

Belinda explained that the tryout was mostly about walking on a leash. "I want to see if Bear can stay on task with entrances and exits. He'll be excited to see Gilbert and Sullivan, but we don't want him to stop moving. If he won't walk by them without stopping to say hi, we won't be able to use him."

Kaylee gave a nod. "Got it."

"For your audition, you and Bear will need to walk to the middle of the stage, pause and count to five, then cross the rest of the way and exit," Belinda said. "Each time it's your cue to cross, Quinn will tap you."

"Quinn?" Kaylee asked.

Belinda pointed toward the young woman who had manned the table. Quinn waved. "My niece and the youngest member of the troupe. She'll be acting as stage manager for the auditions."

Kaylee felt her cheeks warm. She was sure Belinda had said

Quinn's name during the introductions, but Kaylee had been distracted by the mystery surrounding Delia. "Okay," she said. "I think we can do that."

"Great." Belinda smiled brightly. "Go with Quinn, and she'll show you where to stand and help Bear into his costume."

"Costume?" Kaylee echoed.

"It's a little saddlebag-style backpack. Not heavy, but it is part of the whole mistaken-identity gag in the play, so I need to know if he'll wear it." She tapped the polka-dot bow tie Bear was wearing. "I don't think it's a problem since he's clearly used to dressing up, but it's still good to be sure."

"Should I take off the bow tie?"

Belinda paused, clearly thinking it over. "No, not for the audition. He won't be able to wear it in the actual play, but it will be fine for tonight."

"Sounds good," Kaylee said, forcing cheer into her voice. She followed Quinn offstage and was pleased to see Bear didn't mind the backpack as Kaylee strapped it on. Within moments, they were in place and waiting for their cue.

Rhett walked up to stand beside Kaylee with one of the other dachshunds on a leash. The dog offered Bear one sniff, then shifted focus to the stage. Bear's attention went everywhere as he looked at the other dog, at Rhett, at Quinn, and at Kaylee, all with his tail wagging wildly. Kaylee bent to give him a pat, then stood up and took a deep breath as they began.

For the audition, Belinda stayed on the stage watching the action. Delia led the other little dachshund. Kaylee wished she'd asked Rhett which dog he was leading. With them all wearing matching saddlebags, it was impossible to discern one dog from another. The only way to tell them apart was that Bear wagged his tail wildly every time he passed Gilbert or Sullivan. But he kept walking.

In fact, it was Kaylee who nearly messed up, not Bear. During one of her exits, she almost ran into a stagehand dressed in black and standing in the shadows. If Bear hadn't spotted him and pulled Kaylee to the side, she certainly would have collided with the man. Kaylee whispered a quiet apology, but the stagehand didn't say anything. Kaylee felt her face warm as he stared at her. *We probably aren't supposed to talk backstage.*

When the scene finished, Belinda called Kaylee and Bear out after Delia and Rhett had led the other dogs from the stage. Belinda squeezed Kaylee's free hand while the audience clapped wildly. It was clear Bear enjoyed the applause very much.

"He did great. He followed your lead perfectly," Belinda said, causing Kaylee to feel a swell of pride on Bear's behalf. "Now let's have some applause for our other two stars," Belinda called, raising her voice to be heard in the audience. "Gilbert? Sullivan?"

Rhett trotted out from the wings leading one of the dogs. They stopped at center stage and bowed. Kaylee giggled as the tiny dachshund bent his head in a bow to match Rhett's. Then Kaylee realized Rhett was the only one who came out with a dog.

"Delia?" Belinda called. "Bring out Sullivan."

They waited another moment, but when the older woman didn't walk out onto the stage, Belinda, Rhett, and Kaylee rushed to the opposite wing from where Rhett had been standing. They found Delia Putnam lying still as death in the shadows near the backstage rigging.

And Sullivan was nowhere to be seen.

3

After such a dramatic ending to the auditions, Kaylee spent a restless night full of dreams twisted by anxiety. She wished she were the one with Saturday off from work instead of Mary. "Who knows," she said to Bear as they walked out to her red Ford Escape Saturday morning. "Maybe we'll hear good news when we get to the shop. Delia will be fine, and they'll have found Sullivan." They could hope, anyway.

Kaylee was surprised to find the outdoor air a bit warmer than the week had been. Morning sunshine bathed her lawn and lifted her spirits a little.

Though Mary wasn't scheduled to work, Kaylee found her at The Flower Patch when she walked in. "I heard about that little dog at the theater," Mary said as she held up a to-go cup of coffee bearing the logo of Death by Chocolate, the bakery next door that belonged to their friend Jessica. "I thought you might be shaken up, so I picked up a cup of coffee. I've got some pastries to go with it."

"You're a lifesaver. I didn't sleep as well as I'd hoped."

Bear trotted up to Mary and sat, clearly expecting her usual compliment on his jaunty bow tie. Today's featured tiny squirrels and acorns.

"Yes, hello, handsome boy." Mary stooped and patted Bear's head. "Did you actually see the poor actress who passed out?"

"I'm not sure she passed out," Kaylee said as she accepted the cup of coffee Mary offered. "She was still unconscious when the ambulance came and took her away. I stayed to help search for Sullivan, but we couldn't find him. Bear and I drove around the area for a while before we went home, but there was no sign of the poor little guy."

"He may still be inside the theater somewhere," Mary suggested. "That building is huge, and the dog might have been frightened when the woman passed out. Little dogs can be very good at hiding. I think it's too early to panic."

Kaylee shivered at the thought of losing Bear and fought the urge to pick him up and never let him go. *I would definitely be panicking if it was him.* But she appreciated the effort and gave Mary a hug. "Maybe we'll get some good news sometime today."

"That's the spirit. If you need me to stay, I can change my plans. I hate to leave you when you're still upset from last night."

"No, I'm all right," Kaylee insisted. "Besides, Herb would be peeved if I kept you from spending the day with him. Go on. It was nice of you to come by and check on us, but we'll be fine."

"Herb would probably rather you kept me—it'd get him out of shopping," Mary said drily. "But I'll go. I want to get my holiday shopping done early this year. It's probably an unrealistic dream, but I'm going with it. You call if you need me. Don't just try to tough it out. There's no reason for that nonsense."

"Yes ma'am," Kaylee said with a smile. "I hope I hear *something* about Delia or Sullivan. Belinda must be in a state." The poor actress certainly had been the night before. "Did you know that the woman who collapsed was the same one who told us the play wasn't going to happen?"

Mary's concerned expression transformed into surprise. "No, I didn't. So she's actually part of the troupe? Do you have any idea why she would say something so negative?"

"I never had a chance to talk to her," Kaylee said. "Maybe it was only an impulsive comment made when she was annoyed about something. I hope she's going to be all right."

"You'll let me know if you hear anything?"

"Of course." Kaylee shooed her assistant toward the door. "Now go. Shop. Give my love to Herb."

Once Mary left, Kaylee gave in to the urge to check on Bear. Her gaze swept the area nervously until she saw him peering around the end of the counter. *He's fine,* she scolded herself firmly. *I will not overreact.* But despite her resolve, she felt a rush of panic every time Bear was out of her sight. Thankfully Bear didn't mind the extra attention and was content to stick right by Kaylee's side while she cleaned a bit and worked on a couple of small ready-to-buy bouquets to put in the display case.

"There's no band of dachshund thieves running around Turtle Cove," she told herself firmly as she pulled out the notes for the only order she had to fill, an arrangement for an anniversary party. The design was large but not complicated, and Kaylee appreciated the soothing, almost meditative act of selecting the most perfect blossoms from her stock in the cooler.

As she slipped several long-stemmed roses into the damp floral foam, she thought again about the lily Belinda had been holding during the auditions, *Lilium auratum,* also called the golden-rayed lily of Japan or the goldband lily. The blooms were beautiful—mostly white with a yellow stripe on the center of each petal, sometimes covered with orange speckles—but unusual because the stems could grow two to five feet, and she'd even heard of some getting up to eight.

Kaylee tried to think of the last time she'd used a *Lilium auratum.* She'd once had a special request for some of them for a funeral arrangement. *Great, associating the flower with funerals is going to cheer me right up.*

She was so deep in thought that she actually startled when the shop door opened. Bear jumped to his feet to scramble out and greet the customer. Bear had taken on the role of shop greeter, which Kaylee normally found charming and adorable.

Today, however, she wished he was a little less friendly as he darted out of her line of sight.

Kaylee hurried out of the design workroom and immediately recognized Belinda Case patting Bear. She gazed up at Kaylee with swollen, red eyes and spoke in a choked voice. "He looks *so* much like Sullivan." At that point, she broke down sobbing. Since she was still squatting next to him, Bear scrambled up to lick at her chin, clearly offering comfort. *Good boy.* Belinda scooped him up and hugged him as she stood and cried into the scruff of his neck.

Kaylee retrieved a box of tissues, waiting for Belinda to regain her composure. Finally, the actress handed Bear to Kaylee and grabbed some tissues to wipe at her eyes and nose. "I'm so sorry," she said at last. "I didn't mean to fall apart."

"Please don't apologize," Kaylee said as she put Bear on the floor. He sat close to Belinda, as if ready in case she needed him again. "I'd be a complete wreck."

"You're very kind, but I didn't come by to cry all over Bear. I wanted to make sure you were both okay, and to order some flowers for Delia. I'm going to go visit her later today."

"Is she in the hospital?" Kaylee asked. Technically, Orcas Island only had a medical center over in Eastsound, but locals frequently referred to it as the hospital because it was simpler.

"Yes, she's still unconscious. The doctor says every hour that she doesn't wake up is concerning." Belinda's voice choked again. "I've known Delia for years. She's one of my dearest friends. She's the big sister I never had."

Kaylee gently placed a hand on Belinda's arm. "Would you like some tea? Sometimes telling troubles to a friend over a cup of tea is just what's needed to soothe the mind and heart."

Belinda bobbed her head, her eyes still shining with tears. Kaylee led her to the sitting area where she normally did consultations. Belinda sat perched on the edge of the cushions of the love seat, and Bear trotted over to lean against her ankles.

"Do you have a tea preference?" Kaylee asked.

Belinda lifted Bear into her lap. "Maybe a nice herbal."

"You got it."

When Kaylee returned with a tea tray, Belinda acted considerably more composed and Kaylee was grateful for Bear's comforting presence. She sat down beside Belinda and handed her a cup of lemon balm tea.

"We can go through some of my books so you can pick an arrangement for Delia." Kaylee gestured toward a stack of photo albums.

Belinda took a long sip of tea. "That would be good. Can I get something with daisies in it? They're Delia's favorite. When she was a little girl, her mother even called her Daisy."

"That's a sweet nickname." Kaylee pulled out an album that she knew contained photos of several arrangements featuring daisies. "Do the doctors know what happened to Delia?"

"She hit her head, probably when she fell. They can't say why she might have fallen, though. She wasn't sick as far as I'm aware." Belinda took a deep breath. "I'm afraid someone might have attacked her and kidnapped my darling Sullivan."

"What do the police think?" Kaylee asked.

Belinda snorted. "They think she fell and hit her head, and Sullivan ran off. But Sullivan is a well-trained dog. He wouldn't run off."

"He might have been frightened by Delia's fall," Kaylee said gently, though she knew Bear wouldn't run away if Kaylee fell down and knocked herself out. Her brave little dog would guard her to the best of his ability. She was certain of that.

Clearly Belinda believed the same of Sullivan. "He wouldn't run away. He simply wouldn't. Except maybe to get help, and he knew where we were."

"I believe you. You know him best."

"I do. I love both my little doxies, of course, but Gilbert is really Rhett's dog. Sullivan is my boy all the way." Belinda sniffled but didn't break down. "I'm worried that the police aren't taking his disappearance seriously because he's a dog."

Kaylee quickly yet tactfully steered Belinda away from that supposition. "The police on the island are extremely hardworking, and many are dog lovers. They have always shown a great fondness for Bear. You can trust them to do anything and everything in their power to help find Sullivan. The community will as well. Bear and I drove through neighborhoods around the theater before going home last night, and I doubt I was the only one."

"I appreciate that. I'm sure you're right. I'm sorry if I sounded critical." Belinda leaned over Bear to set her cup on the tray, then hugged him again. "I wish Delia would wake up. I hope she's okay, but I also want her to tell me who took my dog. I know it makes me sound self-centered, but I can't help it."

"It makes you sound like someone who loves her dog. That's not a bad thing." Kaylee remembered Delia's ominous prediction about the new playhouse. She didn't want to add to Belinda's distress by mentioning it, but she did ask about the play. "Will you be putting off rehearsals until you find Sullivan and Delia is released from the hospital?"

Belinda shook her head. "The show must go on. That is an adage we take seriously. Which brings me to a question I want to ask you: can Bear stand in for Sullivan until we find him?"

"I suppose," Kaylee said tentatively, feeling a distinct unease about taking Bear to the theater where Sullivan had vanished. "Though I hope it won't be an issue. I'm sure someone will bring Sullivan home very soon."

Belinda reached out to squeeze Kaylee's hand. "I'm so glad

I met you." She took a deep breath, and set Bear gently on the floor before straightening up and tapping the binder in Kaylee's lap. "Now, let's pick some flowers."

Belinda soon chose a nice bouquet, and Kaylee promised to work on it right away. Belinda told her she'd send her niece out to pick up the arrangement later.

"Quinn is lovely, by the way," Kaylee told Belinda. "I was very impressed by how patient she was with everyone as they signed up for auditions."

"She's the best," Belinda agreed. "We're lucky to have her. She's young, but she's going to be a fine actress. And she's a real trouper about the dogs."

"What do you mean?" Kaylee asked.

"She's allergic. She doesn't complain, but I'm not sure her allergy meds are doing the trick."

Kaylee remembered Quinn's red eyes. That was one mystery solved. "I was a little worried when I saw her red eyes. I thought maybe she was upset."

"Well," Belinda said, drawing out the word as if trying to decide whether to tell Kaylee what she knew. "Between us, she's also nursing a bit of a broken heart. She had a boyfriend at our last theater location and things didn't work out. I never trusted the guy, personally, and I think she's better off without him. I'm hoping that coming here will put enough distance between her and her troubles to help her feel better."

"She certainly didn't seem to let it affect her work," Kaylee said, then added, "All of your troupe members seem so nice."

"They're wonderful," Belinda agreed enthusiastically. "We've worked with most of them through many productions. It's good to have a core group that you can trust."

"Trust?"

Belinda nodded. "Actors talk about trust a lot. I suppose

that makes us sound paranoid, but we mostly mean people that we know will step up if there's any kind of unexpected mistake during performances. If someone forgets a line, someone else will fill in so the audience is none the wiser."

"I can see how that would be helpful," Kaylee said.

"In our business it's practically life and death," Belinda said, then she laughed. "There I go again. I guess we actors are simply a dramatic bunch." She reached out and squeezed Kaylee's hand again. "I'm so glad I came in today. Talking to you has made me feel better—as much as anyone could, I suppose. You have a very comforting aura."

Kaylee had never thought much about her "aura," but she was glad she'd helped the actress.

Once Belinda left, the flower shop stayed quiet for the rest of the morning with only a few customers buying small impulse bouquets. That gave Kaylee plenty of time to put together Delia's arrangement, and she was pleased with the result.

When Quinn dropped by, she greeted Kaylee and Bear warmly, kneeling down to pet him. "This guy is so sweet," she announced when Bear put his front paws up on her bent knee.

"He sure is," Kaylee said. "But should you be petting him with your allergies?"

Quinn waved that off as she stood. "I am not going to be ruled by my allergies. *I* run my life, and I love dogs."

Kaylee approved of the young woman's attitude and suspected she would handle her break up with her boyfriend just fine with that kind of spunk.

Quinn surveyed the shop. "This place is so cute. I'm so glad my aunt sent me for the flowers. I'll have to come back soon and shop for something for my room."

"Are you staying at Robin's Nest?" Kaylee asked.

Quinn shook her head. "Only Belinda and Rhett live there.

The rest of us are sharing some rental housing a little ways from the theater. It's not terrible, but it could use some homey touches."

"I'll be happy to make you something for that. Just let me know when you want it," Kaylee said, then retrieved the flowers for Delia.

When Quinn left with her aunt's order, Kaylee faced an empty shop again. She considered putting up a *Be Right Back* sign and taking Bear for a walk. She could use the exercise to ease her worry. About the time she decided to give in to the urge, however, the door opened and Deputy Nick Durham walked in.

Bear gave a joyful bark at the sight of his good friend and scampered over to the deputy so quickly he actually slid on the wood floor. Nick laughed and bent to pet the little dog. "I'm glad to see you too, buddy."

A longtime member of the Orcas Island Sheriff's Department, Nick was a good guy, if a bit of a flirt. When she'd first met him, Kaylee had found his flirting off-putting, but now she realized that was only a small part of Nick's personality—and one that he thankfully never directed at her. He never meant any harm and seemed to know when to stop. He was a smart cop, and he'd become a loyal friend.

"Shopping for a new lady friend?" Kaylee asked him as he stood up.

Nick wrinkled his nose and pulled a notepad from his pocket. "Not this time. I'm interviewing everyone who had an opportunity to be backstage at the theater at the auditions. You're last on my list."

"Have you learned anything helpful?" Kaylee asked.

Nick gave her his most charming grin. "I can't talk about an open case."

Kaylee raised an eyebrow. "You and I both know that doesn't apply to me." She had consulted with the police on numerous occasions, both in Seattle and on Orcas Island."

Nick chuckled. "That does seem to be true, doesn't it?" His grin morphed into a more rueful expression. "Not that I have any secrets to protect. Did you see anything unusual when you were backstage with Bear?"

"I saw a lot of people, but I couldn't tell you exactly who. It was dark back there," Kaylee answered. "I'm afraid I didn't pay as much attention as I could have to the troupe when Belinda introduced them. And she didn't even introduce stagehands, though I saw one. Honestly, I don't think I would have noticed a strange face since they were all new to me."

"I talked to all the actors, and none of them reported seeing anyone suspicious," Nick said. "Of course, they are all actors, so I probably couldn't tell if any of them was lying."

Kaylee had a sudden idea. "Did you talk to the stagehands? I nearly ran into one of them, and he was on the same side of the stage where we found Delia. Maybe he saw something."

Nick frowned. "Everyone I talked to was introduced as a member of the acting troupe. I didn't meet any backstage workers. I'll have to follow up on that."

"Do you have any updates on Delia?" Kaylee asked. "Belinda was in earlier, and she's very worried about her."

"I drove out to the hospital and talked to Delia's doctor. He told me that her scans were negative for swelling in her brain, which is a good sign. Now we wait until she wakes up."

"And search for Sullivan in the meantime."

"Kaylee, I know how much you love dogs. I do too, but we're mostly focusing on the possible assault here. We searched the theater, but we don't have the manpower for a house-by-house search for a dog."

"Is that how you'd act if it was Bear?" Kaylee demanded.

"It's how I would act officially," Nick said gently. "But I'd put my off-duty hours into searching for him, just as I have driven through neighborhoods hunting for Sullivan. I'm already seeing posters up for him as well."

"Thank you. I'm sorry I was sharp." Kaylee relaxed a little. She really shouldn't have doubted her friend.

"I don't blame you. If a dog that looked exactly like my dog went missing, I'm sure I'd be in a similar state."

"So you think Delia was assaulted? Belinda said she fell and hit her head."

"She did, but I find myself wondering why she fell." Nick scratched his chin thoughtfully. "There was no loose floorboard or other obvious hazard. I suppose she could have tripped on the dog's leash, but we have to consider the possibility that she was pushed. We're examining all the options. The fact that there has been no ransom demand for the dog makes us think more and more that this isn't a dognapping. I'm hoping it's a simple accident."

"Me too. That would make me feel much better. Granted, so would Sullivan's safe return."

"It's not as if no one is searching. People all over the island are keeping an eye out because of the news alert. I've been all over that theater, and I can't see any way Sullivan could have gotten outside unless someone opened the stage door for him."

"So you think someone took him?" Kaylee asked.

"It's a possibility. But it's also possible that someone left the stage door open, and he or she isn't owning up to the mistake."

Kaylee fiddled with a pen from the counter, rolling it gently while she tried to decide what to say next. Nick waited patiently, though she could tell the sharp-eyed deputy hadn't missed her fidgeting. He knew her well enough by now to be able to tell when she was deciding something. Finally, she said, "Delia said something odd to me the other day."

"At the audition?"

"No, before that. She was browsing here in the flower shop and overheard Mary and me talking about the play. She said something to the effect that we shouldn't bother with the auditions because the play was going to be a disaster and probably never open."

Nick's eyebrows climbed high on his face. "Did she say why?"

"No. We were caught off guard by that sort of remark from a perfect stranger, and Delia left the shop right after. It wasn't until the audition that I realized she was actually connected with the play."

"Sounds like she might know all kinds of things when she wakes up. I look forward to the conversation we'll have when that happens." Nick bent to give Bear another pat. "I should be going. I want to get back to the hospital. On the way, I thought I'd drive around the side streets near the theater again."

"You're a good guy, Nick." Kaylee scooped up Bear and gave her dog a squeeze. "I think I'll take a break and walk Bear in that direction. Who knows what he might lead me to? Someone had better find Sullivan soon. It's getting cold at night, and that little guy needs to be home."

"I'm with you on that," Nick said. "Don't worry. We'll find him."

Kaylee released a doleful exhale. "I can't tell you how much I want to believe that."

4

Despite Kaylee's hopes and prayers, days went by without any sign of Sullivan. When Kaylee carried Bear into the Old Cape Lighthouse for the Tuesday evening meeting of the Petal Pushers, she found that Sullivan was on everyone's mind. In fact, the play seemed to push flower talk right off the agenda. Even the delicious chocolate goodies Jessica had brought from Death by Chocolate were being ignored.

"Polly and Zoe insisted we drive around hunting for Sullivan before they could settle down after the auditions," DeeDee said as she slowly spun a cup of coffee between her hands, her gaze focused on the mug. "They're just distraught over him, and I have to admit I'm not doing much better."

"I know." Mary sighed. "Every time I get in the car, I do a little extra tour around the neighborhood, searching for him. It's made me aware of how tiny dachshunds truly are. One could hide almost anywhere."

"But he'd have to come out to eat." DeeDee glanced up from her cup. "The fact that he hasn't been found when everyone is searching for him is worrying. And I can't help but wonder..."

"What?" Mary prompted after a moment.

DeeDee bit her lip. "What if that woman's fall wasn't an accident? What if the theater is dangerous? Both of my girls have roles in that play, and I don't know if I should let them continue to participate."

The whole room was quiet for a moment after that. Kaylee wanted to say something comforting, but she carried the same worries herself.

Jessica hopped up, grabbed a napkin and a double-chocolate muffin from the tray, and plopped it in front of DeeDee, then laid a comforting hand on her shoulder. "You won't need to watch over them alone. This community looks out for one another."

"I do know a couple of the people in the street scenes," DeeDee said, then she offered a small smile to Kaylee. "And Bear, of course." In Kaylee's lap, Bear sat up straighter at the sound of his name.

"I have to admit, I've been going back and forth about the play myself." Kaylee stroked Bear's smooth head and velvety ears. "I think it's going to be hard to be completely comfortable until the question of what happened to Delia is solved. And that won't happen until she wakes up."

"When Herb and I were out shopping the other day, I ran into a friend who works as a nurse at the hospital," Mary said. "She told me it's very worrying that Delia is still unconscious. The doctors aren't quite sure why she hasn't woken up. The brain can be a mysterious thing, and doctors don't know everything."

Kaylee thought again about Delia's prediction. If enough people pulled out of the play because of the woman's injury, it might make her prediction come true, though Kaylee doubted that was how Delia had thought it would happen.

DeeDee picked at her muffin absently, before lifting her head and focusing her grayish-blue eyes on Kaylee again. "Rehearsals begin this Thursday. Are you and Bear going to be there?"

Kaylee knew her friend hoped for one more person to help keep the girls safe. "Yes," she said hesitantly, "but I'm taking it one step at a time. If anything feels off, I'm out."

With a whoosh of pent-up breath, DeeDee visibly relaxed. "Same here. I'll bring the girls Thursday, and we'll play it by ear after that. One thing that makes me feel a little better is how nice all the actors were to the girls. They didn't behave as if Zoe and Polly were underfoot or a nuisance. They seemed genuinely excited about having young people interested in acting. Did you meet Belinda's niece, Quinn Selby? She's not much more than a teenager herself, and the girls adored her."

"I did meet her," Kaylee said. "She's very nice. I noticed her eyes were red and wondered if she'd been crying, but her aunt told me she's allergic to dogs. You'd never know it from the friendly way she treated Bear."

"My roommate in college had terrible allergies," DeeDee said. "And her eyes were red about half the time. It didn't make Quinn any less outgoing. She was giggling with Polly and Zoe before their audition, and it definitely helped them be less nervous."

"The theater people do seem kind," Kaylee said. "And I promise to do my part to keep an eye on the girls, though my other eye is going to be for Bear."

DeeDee sat up straighter, as if some of the weight were lifting off her. "We can do this."

Kaylee nodded, trying to reflect DeeDee's optimism.

Mary stood and waved at everyone for attention. "Now, in the spirit of us being a gardening club, we should probably talk a bit about flowers. I fell woefully behind in prepping my garden beds for the change of season. Please tell me I'm not the only one."

"As long as I get it done by Thanksgiving, I figure I'm ahead," Jessica said. "I think this is going to be a cold winter. Oliver's leaves get droopy every time someone opens the shop door."

DeeDee glanced at her sharply. "I thought his drooping was an omen of danger." Kaylee was surprised by DeeDee's reaction. Everyone knew Jessica was convinced her lavender geranium could tell the future, but DeeDee had never shown any sign of buying into the idea.

"I'm certain this is weather-related drooping," Jessica said confidently. "I can tell the difference."

"A cold winter is all the more reason to get the gardens ready," Mary said, pulling the conversation back to gardening.

Everyone seemed willing to let her. The topic of the play was left behind, but Kaylee could tell by DeeDee's lapses into silence and her own unease that neither of them had moved on completely. She scratched Bear under the chin and tried to tamp down her worries. After all, by the first rehearsal, Delia might be awake and Sullivan could be safe and sound at home. She was worried for nothing.

Probably.

Unfortunately, Kaylee walked into the theater Thursday night with a heavy heart, having heard no good news about either Delia or Sullivan. She'd considered driving out to the hospital to check on the actress, but didn't know what good it would do. Since the woman was unconscious and Kaylee wasn't a relative, it wasn't likely Kaylee would even get in to see her.

That's the worst thing, Kaylee thought as she settled into a seat near the stage. *All this worry and nothing to do about it.*

Bear gave a surprised yip as someone plopped into the seat beside Kaylee. "Isn't this exciting?" Polly asked, bouncing in the seat a few times.

Kaylee reached out to tweak the end of the little girl's braid. "It is now. I'm not surprised you and Zoe got roles." She leaned closer. "You two were the best."

"I thought so too," Polly said in her most adult voice. "We practiced."

DeeDee slipped into the row and shooed Polly down one seat so she could sit by Kaylee. Polly started to voice a protest, but her mom shushed her. "It's what you get for running in the theater. I'd better not see any more of that."

"Yes ma'am," Polly said as she settled into her new seat, where she was sandwiched between DeeDee and Zoe. As often happened these days, Zoe looked at her little sister with a disapproving frown.

"I think Bear is nearly as excited as Polly," Kaylee said. "He loves all the people."

"And all the people love him." DeeDee laid a hand on Kaylee's arm. "I totally forgot something I meant to say at the Petal Pushers meeting. Would you and Bear be able to have Thanksgiving with us this year? The girls have been begging me to ask you, and of course Andy and I would love to have you."

Kaylee hadn't given much thought to the looming holiday. With her family living in Florida and Arizona, it was hard to find the time and money to visit them for every Thanksgiving, Christmas, and Easter. "That's very kind of you, I'd love it," she said. "And so would Bear. Just let me know what I can bring."

As DeeDee agreed, Belinda walked onto the stage carrying another one of the long-stemmed lilies. She used it to gesture to the audience. "Thank you all for coming out to our first rehearsal for *Midsummer Madness*. We're excited about the amazing new talent we saw at auditions, but before we jump into the hard work of rehearsals, I have wonderful news." Belinda paused for effect, her eyes sparkling. Finally, she exclaimed, "Delia woke up late last night! She's still pretty blurry on the details of her fall, but her doctors say she's out of the woods. She may even be joining us for this very play." The smile that Belinda gave everyone as they applauded the news was brilliant, but Kaylee noticed Belinda hadn't mentioned Sullivan in her announcement.

Clearly Kaylee wasn't the only one who wondered about Sullivan, as an unfamiliar woman's voice called out from the audience, "What about the dog?"

The actress's glow dimmed a bit. "Sullivan is still missing. I cannot tell you enough how much I appreciate all the community support we've had in the search for my dear little dog." Her voice broke on the last word. She dropped the lily and ran offstage.

A murmur ran through the audience, then Rhett walked out onto the stage and scooped up the flower. "I'm sure everyone can understand Belinda's worry about Sullivan," he said. "We'll give her a few minutes to collect herself. In the meantime, let's get started." He beckoned to Kaylee. "Could we have Bear up here, please? He'll be needed in some of the group scenes. Nothing too strenuous, I promise."

Kaylee stood and felt a supportive pat on her arm from DeeDee as she eased by her. When she and Bear joined Rhett at the front of the stage, Quinn came from offstage to stand on the other side.

"Okay, Quinn is going to work with our younger actors in this first scene," Rhett said, "so could all the kids come up?" Then he leaned closer to Kaylee and lowered his voice. "Come with me."

Once they were offstage, he glanced sideways at her. "You run a flower shop, right? And you know a good bit about flowers?"

Kaylee laced her fingers together, falling easily into academic mode. "My specialty is plant taxonomy."

He shook his head. "I don't know what that is, but it doesn't matter." He held up the lily that Belinda had dropped on the stage. "Did this thing come from your shop?"

"No." Kaylee held out her hand, and Rhett gave her the flower. "I rarely use *Lilium auratum*. They're not easy to get, though I've had a few shipped in for special orders now and again. They would be very expensive this time of year as they have to be grown in a greenhouse because they're out of season. They don't grow well in this climate anyway, and they aren't a small plant."

He gave the flower a disgusted glare. "I hate these things. They stink, and they're too big."

Kaylee thought he seemed awfully worked up over a flower. "I suppose. They are sometimes called the golden-rayed lily because of these gold stripes coming from the center."

He waved that off. "If it didn't come from your shop, do you know where someone might have gotten it? There's been one left in the middle of the stage every day since the first audition. No one can figure out who's doing it."

"A fan maybe?" Kaylee suggested.

"A creepy fan," Rhett grumbled. "At first, Belinda thought it was charming, and she's still trying to be upbeat about it in case it's all well-meaning, but I don't like it. It doesn't feel right."

"I can ask around," Kaylee said. She wasn't the only florist in the area, and other businesses sometimes imported flowers for special events. "Do you think it could be a member of your cast or crew?"

"I've asked everyone," he said. "If it was, I think they would have stopped by now. I've made it clear how I feel, and I am still everyone's boss here."

"How easy would it be for an outsider to leave it?" Kaylee's gaze swept the shadowy backstage. "I don't know which doors lead out of the building."

"There's a stage door," Rhett said, waving vaguely, "but it's locked to the outside. It's easy enough to go out, but you have to turn the lock if you want to get back in. Come on, I'll show you."

Kaylee and Bear followed Rhett. She brought the lily up to her nose and breathed in the spicy aroma. Despite what Rhett had said, Kaylee found the scent pleasant, less unbearably sweet than some lilies could be.

Rhett led her down a dimly lit hallway lined with doors.

"Dressing rooms," he explained. "Your dog won't have a dressing room, though. We reserve these for human actors."

"That's all right. I don't think Bear will be a diva about it," Kaylee joked.

At that, Rhett's stern expression lightened. "I'm glad someone won't be."

When they reached the stage door, Rhett showed her how it locked and unlocked. He held open the door so she could see the scraggly patch of grass killed by the colder temperatures. "I don't think anyone is sneaking flowers through here every morning. They must be coming through the main doors, which are usually open so our actors can get in. We seem far more ready to open than we are, and Belinda isn't above repurposing our players as a painting crew when she needs to."

"I hear a theater troupe can be like family," Kaylee said.

"I guess," Rhett said. "A big, dysfunctional family." He wrinkled his nose again at the flower in Kaylee's hand, then plucked it out of her fingers and threw it outside. The long-stemmed lily made a sharp contrast with the brown grass.

For some reason, the sight of the bruised lily on dead grass reminded Kaylee of how popular the large gold-and-white flowers were in funeral arrangements, sending a chill up her spine. As Rhett let the stage door swing closed, Kaylee shook off the chill. The flowers were also popular in other large, showy displays that needed huge blooms. There was no reason for her mind to go straight to funerals.

I'm being silly and superstitious. She shivered. *At least, I hope I am.*

5

Belinda appeared then, her face pink and gleaming as if she'd just washed it. She strode down the hall, the heels of her boots ringing against the wooden floors. "What are you two doing?" she asked. "We're supposed to be having a rehearsal."

"Sorry." Rhett shoved his hands into the pockets of his jeans. "I was just showing Kaylee around. I thought she might have to take Bear out later."

Kaylee immediately understood that he didn't want to upset his wife further by reminding her that not only was their dog missing, but someone was leaving them large flowers for reasons unknown.

Belinda's frown fell away. "I know the backyard area seems sketchy, but I had our people go over it thoroughly. There are no nails or broken glass. It's safe for little paws."

"Glad to hear it," Kaylee answered. She glanced down at Bear, who panted blithely at her feet. "We may try it out later. But for now, I think he's eager to start rehearsing."

Belinda clapped her hands. "Excellent. Let's go."

Once they reached the stage, Belinda explained the scene they'd be rehearsing. "I lead one of the dachshunds and Rhett leads the other. We keep almost meeting, but little things on the street distract us," she explained. "Do you think Bear will let me walk him?"

"I believe so," Kaylee said. "You've petted and fussed over him. Bear's affections are rather easily bought."

"I don't know," Belinda said as she knelt to give Bear a pat. "I think he recognizes good people." She rose and gestured to the wing. "If you'll wait there, I'll be right over. Bear won't need the backpack for this scene, which is good, because we're missing one." In that instant, Belinda clearly remembered the reason why one of the bags was missing, and raw pain flashed over her face. After a moment, she addressed the rest of the actors who would be standing on the stage. "You each know what you're supposed to be doing in this scene, so stay on task and we'll be fine."

Kaylee walked Bear to the shadowy edge of the stage. She felt a tingle of unease at the memory of Delia sprawled in the shadows only a few feet from where she stood with Bear, but since the dog didn't seem to sense anyone in the wings, Kaylee refused to give in to her nerves.

A few minutes later, Belinda took the leash to start the scene. Kaylee watched with pride from the wings as Bear trotted along beside the actress without incident. He stayed calm and never pulled on the leash or lunged toward the wings for Kaylee. He did wag his tail furiously every time he spotted Gilbert and again whenever Belinda led him toward Kaylee, but otherwise his performance was flawless.

After two run-throughs, Kaylee suddenly felt a hand on her arm and gasped in surprise.

"Sorry," DeeDee whispered. "I decided to watch from here. I could see Polly looking for me in the audience. I didn't want her to get in trouble."

"She and Zoe are doing great," Kaylee said.

"So is Bear."

With DeeDee beside her, Kaylee was able to relax enough to pay attention to the scene itself. It was funny, with Belinda and Rhett almost spotting one another over and over. Kaylee had come to think of Rhett as rather dour and grumpy, but onstage in the scene, he radiated charm and good humor. *He's quite an actor.*

Near the end of the third run, Belinda did one of the

exaggerated turns a little closer to the group of children who were supposed to be playing jacks. Bear stuck his nose under Polly's hand, and she gave him a pat.

Belinda stopped. "No, Polly, don't pet Bear. We don't want him to be distracted by anyone in this scene, and when you pet him, it encourages that." Though Belinda's tone was mild, Kaylee could see the rebuke hit Polly hard, and her face reddened.

"Oh no," DeeDee whispered. "Here come the tears."

Polly swallowed hard and nodded, but she didn't cry. Kaylee and DeeDee released pent-up breaths together, then grinned at each other.

The actors went through the scene two more times. Kaylee wondered how the little girls could stay crouched so long without cramped legs. *Ah, the flexibility of youth.*

Kaylee took a step farther from the stage so she could stretch. Standing still so long was growing uncomfortable. That was when she caught sight of a man standing in the deep shadows, his attention on her. When she met his stare, his gaze shied away, but Kaylee had the distinct impression he had been watching her for a while. At first, she thought he could be the stagehand she'd run into during auditions as he was about the same height and build, but the longer she peered at him, the more she thought he probably wasn't. Still, the staring was a little creepy, and she returned to DeeDee's side.

After rehearsal was over, Kaylee headed for the stage to collect Bear, but was sidetracked by an exuberant Polly and Zoe. "Did you see me?" Polly asked, bouncing on her toes.

"I did," Kaylee said. "And I noticed you're very good at jacks."

Polly beamed. "Zoe is better, but she has to stand around and pretend to argue with Meghan."

Zoe giggled. "Meghan and I fake-argued so much on stage that we're feeling a little grumpy about it."

"No we're not!" A girl with a head of dark curls slung an arm about Zoe's neck. Kaylee assumed this was Meghan. "It was fun having a fake argument. We pretend-argued about all kinds of stuff. Miss Belinda said it doesn't matter what we actually argue about, as long as we keep it quiet enough that we don't distract from the main dialogue. My favorite was pretend-arguing about spaghetti."

"They're worms," Zoe said, waving her hands as she had done onstage. "Creepy worms."

"Strings," Meghan said fiercely, poking Zoe's arm. "Pasta strings."

Both girls dissolved into giggles.

Polly shook her head. "I'd rather play jacks."

"And I'd rather load up my girls and get them home," DeeDee said as she joined them. "Meghan, do you need a ride?"

Meghan shook her head, sending her curls swinging. "Dad's in the audience. See ya, Zoe."

"Bye. Mom, did you see me?" Zoe and Polly launched into a moment-by-moment description of their performances, though their words were nearly unintelligible since they spoke at the same time. DeeDee rolled her eyes, then waved at Kaylee as she herded the girls toward the steps that led down to the audience.

Kaylee went in search of Belinda and Bear. Though a few people still stood chatting on the stage, Belinda was not among them. A wash of worry passed through Kaylee, but she pushed it down. *Don't be silly. They're here somewhere.*

She crossed the stage and slipped into the backstage area on the opposite side. It was empty except for a stool in the shadows where Belinda was perched with Bear in her lap. She was hugging the little dog and crying. When she spotted Kaylee, she quickly collected herself and rose. "Sorry, I should have brought Bear to you so you didn't worry. He did wonderfully."

"I'm glad." Kaylee took Bear as Belinda handed him over. "And I'm glad if he helped you feel any better."

Belinda gave Bear a last pat on the head. "I'm afraid nothing is going to do that until I find Sullivan."

Kaylee understood completely. "Is it all right if I walk Bear outside on the grass a little before I put him in the car? He's been inside for a while."

"Of course." Belinda wiped at one eye with the edge of her hand. "I won't need to lock up for a couple of hours yet. I have to talk to Rhett about some changes to that scene. I think some of the pacing needs to be adjusted to get the laughs."

"I thought it was very clever and funny," Kaylee said. Then she remembered the man in the wings and asked Belinda about him.

"It must have been Mike Mortenson," Belinda said. "He's the only man from our regular troupe who is here tonight other than Rhett." She held out a hand a few inches above her own height. "He's about this tall, with brown hair and hazel eyes." She leaned toward Kaylee and lowered her voice. "His hair is getting thin, and he's sensitive about that."

"That sounds like him," Kaylee said. "He made me a little nervous. He was staring at me."

"Poor Mike. He's a wonderful actor and brilliant with makeup. Honestly, he could be a professional makeup artist if he didn't love acting so much. I've seen him do some amazing transformations. But he's super shy. I expect he wishes he had the nerve to walk up and talk to you."

"Shyness and acting seem an unusual combination."

"They go together more than you'd think," Belinda said. "A lot of actors are socially awkward in real life. Some of the tales of how actors can be stuck-up are actually simply misinterpreting social anxiety. Anyway, Mike's a good guy, I promise."

Kaylee set her dog down on the floor. "I'll take your word for it. I'm going to go ahead and take Bear out now. I'll see you soon."

"Okay. And thanks for letting Bear be in the play."

"I should be thanking you. He's certainly enjoying himself."

With a wave, Kaylee left Belinda and escorted Bear to the backstage door. She shivered at the change in temperature, but was glad to find the chill wasn't bitter. She carefully led Bear around the lily on the ground. She didn't think he would try chewing on it, but she didn't want to take the risk. She couldn't remember whether this particular kind of lily was toxic to dogs, but she didn't want to risk it. Even if it wasn't fatal for him, it was still likely to cause him an upset stomach if he ingested any part of it. She was grateful that he wasn't a cat, as all lilies were toxic to them, and they were much less biddable than her usually obedient dachshund.

Bear trotted over to the worn picnic table and snuffled around it. Up close, Kaylee realized the table was in terrible shape, listing decidedly to one side. *I wouldn't dare sit on it.* At the very least, she'd end up with dirty clothes and maybe splinters.

Bear moved past the table, pulling Kaylee farther and farther from the backstage door. "Let's not go so far," Kaylee told him, but Bear continued to pull and strain against the leash. When Kaylee resisted, he stared up at her and barked. "Have you been saving up a couple hours' worth of naughty?" She could tell the only way he'd quit is if she picked him up and carried him, which wouldn't make for much of a walk. "Okay, fine. We'll go your way."

Once she gave in, Bear hurried along at a steady clip as if he had a clear destination in mind. Now and then, he would stop and sniff, but only for a moment before pressing on.

"Where are we going?" Kaylee asked. This was not the best part of town, and she began to feel a little nervous about wandering around at night as they continued well past the lights of the theater.

The smell of old fish and saltwater increased, as did the sound of waves, indicating that they were moving closer to the ocean. This was the working part of the waterfront, and there was nothing touristy about it, including the poor lighting.

"Okay, I've humored you enough. I'm getting cold," Kaylee said, hauling Bear to a stop and bending to pick him up. That was when she heard it—a faint bark in the distance, sounding so much like Bear's that she'd almost believe he'd become a little canine ventriloquist.

Bear barked in response and dodged Kaylee's grab, jumping forward so hard and fast that he was able to pull the leash right out of Kaylee's hand.

"Bear, no!" she shouted, but the little dog dashed away, trailing the leash behind him. Kaylee ran after him, struggling to keep an eye on Bear and the leash in the gloom of the dark waterfront. She made a couple grabs for the leash but missed both times. "Bear, stop!"

To her surprise, he did. But only because they'd reached his destination, a small shed with a battered wooden door. Bear pawed at the door and barked. Wild barking came from the other side.

Kaylee scooped up Bear and examined the door carefully. The latch that held it closed was fastened with a shiny lock, the only new thing about the building. "Do you think that might be Sullivan?" she asked Bear. He yipped in reply.

"It could be where someone keeps their watchdog," Kaylee said. Though she couldn't imagine the yapping bark belonged to a particularly frightening watchdog. It still sounded like it belonged to Bear's twin. "Fine. We need to see this dog."

She tucked Bear under one arm and pulled out her phone. To her relief, she had a strong signal and quickly called both Nick and Reese Holt, Orcas Island's favorite handyman. She explained where she was and why she needed them. She held

Bear close as she waited in the dark for her friends, glad of his small warm body close to hers.

The two men arrived at almost the same time. Reese strode up with a heavy pair of bolt cutters over one shoulder. Kaylee felt her tension ease at the sight of her good friend, whose calm demeanor tended to soothe frayed nerves.

"Are you okay, Kaylee?" Reese asked.

Kaylee bobbed her head. "Just a little nervous standing in the dark. I see you came prepared."

"I could have handled it myself," Nick said as he eyed the bolt cutters.

"I was a little anxious out here all by myself," Kaylee said. "I figured if I called you both, I might get company quicker."

"Reasonable thinking," Reese said, flashing her a disarming smile. "Though you had a bear protecting you. I don't know how much more you'd need."

As if he understood the handyman's words, Bear released a bark of agreement.

Nick rolled his eyes before pointing at the shed. "Do you think that's the actress's dog?" Inside they could hear more barking.

"Well, Bear is fond of Sullivan," Kaylee said, "and he led me right here."

Reese held up the bolt cutters. "I can get us inside."

"Let me make a call before we go tearing up someone's property," Nick said. "But I'm suspicious. We checked this area when the dog first disappeared. I remember this shed. The door hung open then, and there was no dog inside." Nick pulled out his phone and walked a few feet away to give himself a little privacy.

Reese reached out to ruffle Bear's ears. "You still playing hero, old buddy?"

Kaylee could tell by the dog's wriggling that he was wagging his tail. Kaylee felt much better with Reese and Nick there, and clearly Bear did too.

In a few moments, Nick returned. "Apparently this shed is on public land, and it shouldn't have a lock. I guess you can have at it, Reese."

Reese's bolt cutters chewed through the shank on the shiny metal lock with ease. He hauled open the door to reveal a dachshund inside.

Kaylee put a squirming Bear down, and the dogs greeted one another with joy. Inside the shed were a shiny metal food bowl, a water dish, and the little saddlebags that the dog had been wearing when he disappeared. Kaylee pointed at the backpack. "That proves it. This is Sullivan."

Nick snagged the strap on the backpack with a pen and lifted it up, peering at it in the glow from a small flashlight. "This adds weight to the dognapping theory. I'd better call Mrs. Case. You and Bear can go if you want."

Kaylee crossed her arms over her chest for warmth. "If you don't mind, I want to stay until Sullivan and Belinda are reunited. I think it will make Sullivan feel better if Bear stays with him."

The two dogs had flopped down on the boardwalk, practically laying on one another. Reese shucked off his jacket and offered it to Kaylee.

She held up a hand. "No, thank you. You'll be cold."

"Not in this." He plucked at his thick fisherman's knit sweater, a change from his usual T-shirt and flannel shirt. "You need to put another layer on before your teeth start chattering."

Kaylee gave in and slipped into the jacket. It was still warm from Reese's body heat, and Kaylee found it heavenly. She noticed Reese also took up a position beside her where he could act as a bit of a windbreak.

Nick raised an eyebrow. "I guess you're staying too, Reese?"

"If Kaylee is going to wait, so will I."

"Suit yourself." Nick pulled on thin gloves as he leaned into the shed again and picked up something that clung to a rough board on one wall. "Kaylee, can you give me your expert opinion on this?"

She walked over and peered at Nick's open palm. In it lay a piece torn from a flower. Though it was severely wilted and limp, Kaylee could see right away that it had come from some kind of lily. "I'm not sure what variety," she told him. "But it might be from a *Lilium auratum*."

He gave an admiring whistle. "Good job. I can barely tell it's a plant. What makes you think it's that particular kind?"

"Well, someone has been leaving goldband lilies, *Lilium auratum*, on the stage at the theater. Apparently the first one appeared the day of the auditions—the day that Delia was injured and Sullivan disappeared."

"An interesting coincidence," Nick said. "Does anyone know who is leaving the flowers?"

"Rhett Case doesn't seem to, and he's getting pretty annoyed about it." Kaylee pointed at the scrap of plant. "I could identify that for sure if I could examine it under a microscope. It's a fairly large piece."

"If this is a fairly large piece, I'd hate to see what you'd consider small." Nick laughed. "Okay, if the sheriff decides we need to treat this as a crime, we may be calling on you. In the meanwhile, I'll pack this up as evidence." He gestured at Sullivan, who was still pressed against Bear. "Someone could simply have found Sullivan wandering and shut him up until they could locate the owner."

"I'm not sure how likely that is," Kaylee said. "Everyone I've seen has been talking about the missing dog. You said you've seen the posters. They have a phone number."

"You'd be amazed at how easy it is for people to miss the

obvious," Nick said. "Some of our residents make a point of not knowing what goes on around them. They come to Orcas Island to play hermit, and they do it well. Again, we'll see what the sheriff says."

"Speaking of people talking, has Delia said anything yet?" Kaylee asked. "Belinda told me she'd woken up."

Nick dropped the scrap of lily into an envelope and sealed it. "I talked to her this morning. She thinks she was pushed, but she was pretty vague. She didn't see anyone."

Kaylee nodded. "Belinda said she was still a little foggy."

"More than a little," Nick said. "I would recommend taking anything she says with a grain of salt. She might get clearer after she has more recovery time."

Kaylee murmured a quiet agreement, but inside she thought it might be time she brought some flowers to the woman in the hospital.

"Sullivan!" The shout of joy was met with barks from both dachshunds as Belinda rushed into the shed. She scooped up Sullivan and hugged him close as the little dog bathed her chin in kisses. "I was so worried! Are you okay, sweetie?"

"He seems uninjured," Kaylee said, smiling at the reunion. "Maybe a little tired."

Belinda's eyes shone with tears. "Thank you so much for finding him."

"It was Bear," Kaylee said. "He either heard him barking or sniffed him out, but he led me right here after the rehearsal."

"Well, I'll have to bring Bear a treat. A big one." Belinda laughed through her tears as she held Sullivan close.

Nick had picked up the backpack again and was checking it closely.

"Could I take that with me?" Belinda asked. "I can see it's a little torn, but I'm sure I can get it mended in time for the show."

Nick frowned slightly. "Normally, I'd say no since it's evidence, but I'm not sure what it's evidence of. If this was a dognapping, I still can't imagine why. You never got any contact asking for money, did you?"

She shook her head. "Maybe someone simply wanted a dachshund? Sullivan is purebred."

"We haven't gotten word of any other purebred dogs disappearing." Nick turned the canvas saddlebags over in his hands. "It's a mystery. But I don't think we could find any fingerprints on this rough surface, so we could probably give it to you. Let me take it tonight, but I'll tell the sheriff you want it back as soon as possible."

"I'd appreciate that." Belinda squeezed her dog again. "Can I take Sullivan home? I know Gilbert will be glad to see him."

Nick's attention was back on the saddlebags, and he answered absently. "Sure. Say, do you ever put things in these pockets?"

"No. The saddlebags are strictly for looks. The dogs could balk if there was added weight."

Nick opened one of the small compartments on one side of the backpack. "There's something in here now." He used a pair of tweezers to pull out a folded piece of paper.

"How odd." Belinda leaned closer. "I've never put anything in the pockets."

Nick unfolded the paper, and they all peered at the neat block letters.

Your Number One Fan—Forever.

6

"Our Bear saves the day again," Mary announced the next morning at the flower shop after Kaylee had related the events of the night before. Bear sat up at the sound of his name. "I'd say that deserves a treat."

At that enticing word, Bear's tail wagged so hard his whole body vibrated, making his red plaid bow tie bob under his chin.

"Well, since you've said the T-word, I don't suppose I can play the bad guy now," Kaylee said. "But don't sneak him more than one. I suspect Belinda is going to be by with a big reward eventually."

"As well she should." Mary crossed her arms over her chest. "So what does Nick say? Are they going to track down whoever attacked that poor woman and stole the dog?"

"They still aren't sure anyone did. Apparently Delia says she was pushed." Kaylee paused and took a sip from her mug of coffee. "Which reminds me—I'm planning to take her some flowers and talk to her."

Mary leaned on the front counter. "You don't trust the sheriff's department to do the job?"

"Of course I trust them," Kaylee said. "But I'll feel better if I'm asking questions too. With Sullivan home, Bear won't have a role in the play, but he's still an understudy. Plus, DeeDee's kids are in the cast. I want to be sure the theater is safe, and nothing about this feels safe right now."

"I'll be glad to watch the shop while you take flowers to that actress." Mary beamed at Bear. "And our little hero can stay here with me, where I can tell him how wonderful he is." Bear responded to that with an agreeable bark. "Since you'll be out, could you pick up a roll of stamps for me, please? I was going to run to the post office on a break today, but if you don't mind, that would save me a trip."

"I'd be happy to," Kaylee said, then prepared to leave for the hospital. Though the walk to her car was more than a little nippy, the drive to Eastsound was lovely. The day was bright and clear, and the lighter traffic was a sure reminder of the fast-approaching winter. The abundant Douglas firs meant Kaylee passed plenty of evergreen trees on her route, but now and again she spotted a mature oak that sported a few crimson leaves clinging to mostly bare branches.

At the hospital, Kaylee found Delia napping alone in her room, a bandage wrapped around her head. Kaylee couldn't tell where the specific injury happened. Disappointed that she obviously wasn't going to get to chat, Kaylee walked to the table beside the bed and put her arrangement next to the one she'd made for Belinda.

"You're the florist." Delia's voice was raspy, startling Kaylee.

Noticing that the injured woman was blinking against the room's bright lighting, Kaylee asked, "Do you want me to lower the lights a little?"

"That would be nice." Delia nudged a magazine that lay near her hand. "I thought I would read for a while, but it made my head hurt, and then I fell asleep."

Kaylee walked over to the wall near the door and slid the dimmer to soften the lights. "I hope you're feeling better overall."

"Quite a bit." Delia fumbled for the bed remote and raised herself to near sitting. "At first my head hurt all the time, but it's much better now. I'm mostly a little weak, but the doctor says that will pass." She gestured vaguely toward the flowers. "It was nice of you to deliver the flowers. Who are they from?"

"They're from me," Kaylee said. "I know we don't know one another, but I've been praying for your recovery. Everyone was so glad when you woke up."

Delia smiled. "That's nice. Turtle Cove seems such a friendly town. I've worked auditions before that were like herding grumpy cats, but the people around here are much more agreeable. Well, right up until my fall."

"If you don't mind my asking, how *did* you fall?"

"That handsome policeman asked the same question." Delia's eyes sparkled a little and Kaylee suspected Nick's charm had been at work. "He told me Sullivan was home safe and sound. You don't know how guilty I felt when I woke up and learned that dear little dog was missing. Poor Belinda, she was clearly a mess about it when she visited yesterday. I hope she forgives me."

"I don't think she ever blamed you," Kaylee said.

"Maybe not, but I blamed me, though I would never intentionally let anything happen to Gilbert or Sullivan."

"You aren't to blame. No one takes a hard fall on purpose."

Delia frowned. "I was pushed. I am not sure anyone believes me, but I was. Even that nice policeman wasn't convinced. I could tell."

"I saw a stagehand in the shadows not far from where you fell backstage. Do you know the man's name? Maybe he saw something."

Delia blinked a few times, clearly surprised by what Kaylee said. "You must be mistaken. There were no stagehands on audition night."

"Maybe you just didn't see him?" Kaylee suggested. "The only reason I did was because I nearly ran into the poor man."

Delia began to shake her head, then winced and stopped. "No, you don't understand. Belinda hasn't hired any stagehands yet as far as I know. Apparently Rhett insisted on it. It's a cost-cutting measure during the early rehearsals."

Kaylee was alarmed by this news. "Maybe you should tell *that* to Nick. He may want to follow up since I definitely saw a man backstage."

"I'm not sure if it's worth telling him," Delia said. "I didn't see anyone." She leaned forward slightly and spoke quietly. "Not that I would have. I'm horribly nearsighted, and it's worse in dim light. Besides, as I said, I'm not sure the deputy believes anyone attacked me."

"Doubting everything is the nature of the job for a policeman, I suppose." Kaylee's gaze swept the room. "Can I get you a drink of water?"

"Thank you. That would be nice."

"I've been thinking about what you said the first day I saw you at The Flower Patch," Kaylee said as she poured water from a plastic pitcher into a small foam cup. "You said the show wasn't going to happen. Why is that?" She set the pitcher back on the side table and handed the cup to Delia.

"Thank you." Delia took a long sip. "Nothing mysterious. The Cases have been fighting a lot lately. They've always been prone to big passionate rows, then they sulk a couple days and it's all great again. But lately they've been snippy and mean to one another whenever they're not in public. They're making each other miserable. It feels like the end of the relationship to me, which was why I said the show was going to be a disaster and wouldn't even happen. I shouldn't have said it, but the whole thing has had me sick with worry."

"What do you think is causing the problem?"

Delia took another sip of water, clearly thinking it over. "Money, maybe. Isn't that supposed to be the number one stressor on marriages?"

"That renovation must have been expensive."

Delia nodded, fidgeting with the foam cup in her hands. "Belinda always acts as if they're made of money. I think she has a trust fund or something. I've never asked the specifics, but we're one of the best-funded troupes I've ever worked with."

"So why would they argue about money?"

Delia shrugged. "I don't know. Rhett was suddenly questioning every expense, even normal things, and it was clearly annoying Belinda to no end. And I know for certain that he had been going behind her back and changing decisions she'd made, swapping in less expensive choices."

Kaylee pondered that for a moment while Delia quietly continued to sip her water. "Last night, when we found Sullivan, there was a note in the saddlebag. It said, 'Your Number One Fan—Forever.' I wonder if it might be tied to the flowers that have been appearing on the stage."

Delia lowered the cup, her face full of surprise. "Those flowers are still showing up?" She wrinkled her nose. "Sounds creepy, especially with a note like that. Wasn't there a movie once about a crazed fan?"

"More than one, probably. So you don't know who it could be?"

"We haven't been here long enough to generate an obsessive fan," Delia said. "I would think we'd need to do at least one show, unless it's some wacko who followed us from the mainland."

"Did anything odd happen before you came here?"

"Sure. Fans can be strange." Delia set her cup down on the stand beside the bed. "It's a hazard of being an actor, and it's especially common with beautiful ones like Belinda. Still, there was never any *real* problem."

Until now. Kaylee was pondering what to ask next when Delia's face brightened.

"I remember something Elliot said about the flowers," the actress said. "It was funny and dramatic—classic Elliot."

"Who is Elliot?"

"Elliot Wythe," Delia said. "He's one of the actors in the troupe. Older with white hair. He's a sweetheart, but he's constantly pontificating on something or other. I remember he said that maybe they were ghost lilies. He's wild about the supernatural and always insists every theater we play in is haunted."

"Even one that was newly made?" Kaylee asked.

"It's in a historic building," Delia said. "Elliot eats up history and then concocts ghost stories to go with it. He's a funny old fella."

"He sounds like quite a character." Kaylee made a mental note to chat with Elliot. "So you can't think of anyone who might have an unhealthy obsession with your theater troupe or any member of it?"

Delia didn't answer right away. Instead she seemed focused on the sheet that covered her legs and gently smoothed it with her hands. Kaylee waited quietly, giving the woman the space to decide if she wanted to share. She'd already been unusually open about the theater, but Kaylee wouldn't be surprised if she'd hit a wall.

Finally, Delia leaned toward Kaylee and spoke in a whisper. "Mum's the word?"

"If I can."

Delia frowned for a moment at Kaylee's answer, then said, "I don't *know* anything, you understand, but I get kind of a weird vibe from the new guy. He's never actually performed with the troupe. He's apparently an old friend of Rhett's, or maybe Belinda's—I don't remember offhand."

"Which actor is the new guy?" Kaylee asked.

"Mike Mortenson. He apparently came backstage at our last play on the mainland and talked his way in to see Belinda and Rhett. The next thing I know, he's joining the troupe. That's not exactly unheard of, but it's a little weird. The timing is especially odd."

"Because he showed up at a play?" Kaylee guessed.

Delia shook her head. "Because he still wanted to join when he found out we were coming here. This theater is hardly a sure thing. This is a pretty small town, and the population plummets when the tourists leave. Plus, we're picking a terrible time to open. We should have planned this around summer."

Kaylee had thought the same. "Belinda told me she wanted to build up community support before the tourists return in force. She thought locals would be more forgiving than someone who's just passing through if the theater had growing pains while you get started."

"Yeah, she told us that too. And it might be good thinking, but it feels risky. I guess I understand why Rhett is worried about money. I'm worried about money too."

"So your weird vibe," Kaylee said, bringing the topic back to Mike. "It's mostly about timing?"

"No, there's more. Mike doesn't talk much, but he seems to constantly be underfoot. I can't count the number of times I've nearly run into him lurking in weird places. It's creepy."

"So he might be the number one fan?"

Again, Delia shrugged. "Maybe. He hasn't seemed particularly focused on Belinda or anyone else, but he's always watching. Like I said, it's creepy. I don't know how else to describe it."

So was the note. Kaylee decided she needed to learn more about Mike Mortenson.

"Then there's Quinn's ex," Delia continued.

"Belinda's niece?"

Delia nodded. "One of the reasons she came with us to the island was because she had a messy breakup with some guy."

"Right," Kaylee said. "Belinda told me about that."

"Belinda doesn't know all the details, though," Delia said. "Quinn didn't want to worry her. Quinn told me the guy was possessive, and I think she was scared of him. Honestly, she didn't relax until we came over on the ferry. Quinn didn't tell him where she was going, but that doesn't mean he couldn't find out."

"But why would he attack you?" Kaylee asked. "Or grab Sullivan, for that matter."

Delia shrugged. "Why do creeps do anything?"

Kaylee felt the tingle of unease in her stomach. *Why indeed?*

7

Since she was already in Eastsound, Kaylee decided to do a little more sleuthing. The pet dishes in the shed with Sullivan had been metal and appeared brand-new, but the only pet dishes anyone could buy in Turtle Cove were cute and touristy. Wondering where they'd come from, Kaylee decided to check out the pet store in Eastsound. If they didn't have that type of dish either, then someone had brought pet dishes from the mainland, and that suggested the person had planned to grab Sullivan all along.

Though a considerably bigger town than Turtle Cove, Eastsound made a concerted effort to keep the same kind of seaside charm. The sidewalks were wide, and the shops nearly all featured clapboard siding and lots of windows. Some had wide porches to give them a welcoming country vibe. Here and there, small maple trees offered shade in the summer and a spot of gold and orange flame in the fall, though Kaylee noticed that the little trees had lost most of their leaves.

The shop Kaylee planned to visit, Pet Project, didn't have one of the lovely porches, but it had plenty of clapboard as well as a large whimsically painted sign featuring dogs and cats in a fishing boat.

The chilly air nipped at her as she hurried up the sidewalk from her parking space down the block. She steeled herself against the cold and the slim chance she'd be able to track down the buyer of two fairly generic pet dishes, but she thought she'd try anyway. As far as she knew, this was the biggest pet store on the island and the closest to Turtle Cove.

As she walked into the shop, she could hear barking come from somewhere near the rear. "Someone sounds excited," she said to the young woman at the cash register.

The cashier tucked a strand of long, blonde hair behind one ear. "We do pet grooming," she explained. "Someone is always excited."

"I've got a dachshund with short hair, so he's not too high-maintenance," Kaylee said. "At least when it comes to baths, anyway."

The young woman chuckled. "Lucky you."

"Could you tell me where to find dog dishes?" Kaylee asked, getting to the point of her visit.

"Sure. Aisle 7."

Kaylee found the aisle quickly, then scanned the shelves until she found metal bowls that exactly matched the ones she'd seen at the shed. She carried one up to the register. "Could I ask you something about these dishes?"

"It's stainless steel," the girl volunteered. "It's rust resistant and doesn't hold odors or bacteria the way plastic will. They *are* prone to tipping, though, unless you buy the stand they fit in. I would recommend the no-tip version with the wide base."

"Thanks," Kaylee said. "But I was actually wondering if you've sold any of these in the last week."

The girl shrugged. "We sell pet dishes all the time. I don't pay close attention to what people buy when they shop here."

"Would whoever does the stocking know if any sold in the last week?" Kaylee asked, though she wasn't sure how helpful that would be since the person probably wouldn't know who bought them.

"Sorry, no idea," the checker said. "And I'm not sure why everyone is so worked up about these bowls." She pointed at the bowl in Kaylee's hand. "You're the second person today to ask questions about that dish. The first one was a cop." She narrowed her eyes at Kaylee. "Are you a cop? You don't look like one."

"I'm not." Kaylee had a pretty good idea which officer of the law had been asking questions about the bowls. It appeared she and Nick were thinking along similar lines. "Thanks for your time."

After returning the bowl to the shelf, Kaylee walked out of the shop and shivered in the cold breeze coming off the water a few blocks away. *I'm so glad we found Sullivan. This is no day to be locked in a shed along the waterfront.*

Her gaze swept the surrounding shops as she considered what to do next. Should she head back to Turtle Cove? Then she remembered Mary's request for stamps. She considered driving to the post office since she was slightly underdressed for the weather, but then she had a change of heart. *I'll walk fast and warm up that way.* She trotted down the sidewalk in the direction of the post office.

Her brisk stride kept her from freezing, but she was still grateful for the warmth that wrapped around her as she pulled open the post office door. There was a line at the counter. *Oh well, more time to warm up.*

While she waited, she examined a bulletin board on one wall and admired the flyer advertising new postage stamps coming out soon. She'd always thought of stamps as tiny bits of art, and she often chose carefully whenever buying stamps for her own correspondence. *Not that I send many letters anymore.* She thought of how disappointed her late grandfather had been in the way e-mail had replaced letters, and Kaylee was careful to send real mail once in a while, even if only for birthdays and holidays.

She was so caught up in thoughts of her grandfather that she almost missed a remark made by one of the women in line ahead of her. Only the mention of Turtle Cove pulled her attention to the present.

"It doesn't make sense," a tall, thin woman said to her shorter companion. "Why open a theater in such a dinky little town?"

"It's crazy enough that they picked Turtle Cove," the second woman said, shifting a stack of packages in her arms. "But why November? That's crazy. No one is going to come. Do people in Turtle Cove even care about live theater?"

Kaylee frowned at that. *We're no less cultured because we live in a smaller town.*

"The only thing I can think of," the tall woman said, "is that Eastsound already has plenty of entertainment choices. Maybe the owners of the theater thought Turtle Cove would be grateful to have anything."

The remark made her companion laugh, setting the packages wobbling. Kaylee felt her face warm with annoyance. She almost cut in with a comment or two in defense of Turtle Cove, but swallowed down the urge. *What's the old saying? Don't eavesdrop, or you won't enjoy what you hear.* She supposed she'd proven that.

As the two women moved to the front counter, their discussion of the theater dropped, and Kaylee was left thinking about the valid questions they'd raised. It didn't make sense to her that the Cases were opening a theater in Turtle Cove in November. It didn't seem like solid business judgment, and she wondered if there was something else at play.

She was still musing over it after she'd bought Mary's stamps and headed outside into the cold. The walk to her car was going to be chilly, so she started off at a steady clip across the post office parking lot. As she got closer to her Escape, she was delighted to spot Reese coming out of a hardware store nearby. He seemed to see her at exactly the same time, and his face lit up.

She waved, and Reese trotted across the street to meet her on the sidewalk. "What brings you out on such a chilly day?"

he asked, pushing a hank of sandy brown hair back out of his blue eyes.

"I came to visit Delia in the hospital, and I picked up some stamps for Mary." A brisk breeze swept by, ruffling her hair and making her shiver. "And now I'm thinking of running all the way to my car. I can feel winter coming today."

"No doubt. How about some soup?" he asked. "There's a great place called Souper Hero about a block north of here."

"That sounds wonderful," Kaylee agreed enthusiastically. As they set off up the street, Kaylee noticed that lots of other pedestrians were braving the cold. "I'm surprised to see so many people out on such a blustery day."

"Well it *is* November, the beginning of the holiday season," Reese said. "And Eastsound is the biggest town on the island. I expect people are starting their Christmas shopping."

Kaylee gaped at him in surprise. "I hadn't thought of that. I haven't given a single thought to Christmas. When I lived in Seattle, I'd be bombarded with Santas and Christmas carols by now." She admired the shop windows they passed and saw that holiday decorations were beginning to creep in, though the shops of Orcas Island seemed to hold off longer on going Christmas-crazy than businesses on the mainland.

"I know," Reese said. "Your grandmother used to grumble about how Christmas was drowning out Thanksgiving, and you know how much Bea loves Thanksgiving."

"That she does," Kaylee said, realizing that she hadn't given her grandmother much thought in the last few days. With Bea's favorite holidays coming up, Kaylee thought she really should call her.

"You seem sad," Reese said. "Is something wrong?"

"Not sad so much as pensive," she said. "I think the holidays snuck up on me. DeeDee asked me if I wanted to spend

Thanksgiving with them, which should be fun, but I feel bad about being so unprepared for the holiday season."

"I'd be just as bad if my holiday plans weren't made for me," he said. "I'm heading to California for Thanksgiving. I promised my mom." He raised his eyebrows. "I expect I may be guilted into making the same trip for Christmas, though I keep pointing out that two trips to California in a month is above and beyond the call of family duty. Hey, you want to spend Christmas with us in California?"

Kaylee smiled. "I wasn't trying to drum up sympathy invitations."

"It wasn't a sympathy invitation," Reese said. "I'd enjoy having you along, and my mother would love having one more person to show off her hostess skills for. She has my sister, of course, but she thinks I'm a bit of a barbarian and don't fully appreciate everything she does."

"That's a lovely offer," Kaylee said noncommittally. "Let me think about it."

"Take your time. Mom will be delighted whether she expects you or not." He stopped suddenly and swept a hand toward the front of a small building, clad in the ubiquitous clapboard. "And here we are for lunch."

"Just in time," Kaylee said. "I was beginning to lose feeling in my fingers."

Reese held the door open for her and they slipped inside. At the head of a long buffet-style counter, a large signboard listed their day's soup offerings, as well as drinks and side options. The cozy seating area was about half full of diners.

When they were seated with their lunch, Kaylee sipped her chicken noodle soup, appreciating the warm trail it made inside her on the way down. "Yum. This was a great suggestion."

"I eat here a lot," he said. "Especially in the winter. There is nothing like soup to chase away the cold."

Kaylee made an agreeable noise as she spooned in another bite of hearty soup. The golden broth was stuffed with ample amounts of vegetables, savory chunks of chicken, and plenty of noodles. She knew it wasn't exactly health food with the substantial salt content, but it felt positively restorative after the cold outside.

"I didn't realize you knew Delia well enough to visit her in the hospital," Reese said after a while.

"I don't," Kaylee confessed. "I mostly wanted to know what's going on at the theater."

Reese set his spoon down on a folded napkin and cocked an eyebrow at her. "You're not putting yourself in danger, are you?"

"No more than I am by letting Bear actually be in the play." Kaylee savored another bite, then continued. "In a way, what I'm doing is being sure I'm not putting Bear in danger, and me along with him."

"I can see the reasoning behind that," Reese said in a slightly grudging tone. He set his empty bowl on the tray, then put his spoon inside. "I think I'd feel better if you weren't doing your sleuth thing all by yourself."

"My sleuth thing?" Kaylee's lips quirked up into a small smile.

Reese gave a small shrug and matched her smile. "That's right, Plantsy Drew."

Kaylee rolled her eyes, but chuckled. "That's a new one."

"Thanks, I thought of it myself. Anyway, how about I follow you back to Turtle Cove and we drop by the theater? That way you can chat with some of the other members of the troupe, and I can know you aren't doing it alone."

"I'm not sure that would be well received," Kaylee said. "I don't have an excuse to simply drop by. Believe me, I've tried to think of one."

Reese fussed absently with his napkin, folding it and unfolding it with his brow furrowed in thought. Suddenly he straightened in the seat, his eyes bright. "I've got it."

"I'm all ears."

"I worked a bit on the remodel. The Cases actually tried to convince me to sign on as the general handyman for the theater, but I'm busy this time of year with everyone getting their properties ready for winter. And as soon as the bad weather hits, I'll be swamped, so I didn't think I could make such a large commitment on top of that."

"That makes sense. How does that help us today?" Kaylee asked.

"I could drop by and say I've decided to give the handyman offer a try, with limited hours," he replied. "I could talk about options with the Cases while you discuss all the other things you have in mind with the rest of the troupe."

"I hate to have you say you might be the handyman when you know you can't." Kaylee appreciated Reese's desire to help, but she didn't want to put him in a position of being even a little dishonest.

"Truthfully, I wouldn't mind the work even if I can't commit to being full-time," Reese said. "And I'll tell them that. I can come in during rehearsals and do whatever they need then. Plus, that will let me be there if you, Bear, or DeeDee's girls need me."

"I have to admit that I would feel much better if you're there."

Reese grinned at her. "That's the idea."

Kaylee finished her last bite and sat back with a contented sigh. "All right. I'm ready when you are."

Reese insisted on walking Kaylee to her car before heading to his own. As she was climbing into the SUV, he said, "Wait here while I get my truck. That way we can stay together in traffic on the way to the theater."

"Sounds like a plan," she said. "I'll just crank up my heater and thaw my bones." As he jogged off, Kaylee closed the car door and pulled out her phone to call Mary.

"How goes the sleuthing?" Mary asked when she answered.

"Not altogether successful," Kaylee said. "But I did run into Reese and got some lunch."

"Oh, wonderful." Kaylee detected the gleeful tone in Mary's voice. Her friend wasn't above a little matchmaking, no matter how often Kaylee insisted that she and Reese were just friends. Mary and the rest of the Petal Pushers clearly hoped the friendship would grow into more and frequently teased Kaylee about it.

"Which brings me to my question," Kaylee said, keeping the conversation on the matter at hand. "Reese said he'd go by the theater with me so I can talk to the rest of the actors." She explained about Reese's offer to be part-time handyman for the theater.

"Good idea," Mary said. "Especially since it will mean you're not there alone."

"Then you don't mind if I'm a little later than I planned?" Kaylee sighed. "Actually, a lot later, since I'm already a little later."

Mary laughed. "It's not a problem. We're not busy, and Bear is great company, as always. We'll hold down the fort."

"You're a gem."

Reese's black Ford pickup pulled up beside Kaylee as she hung up. Reese waved at her, and she waved back, then pulled out of her parking space after him.

As she followed him down the street, Kaylee found that she was grateful Reese would be with her when she returned to the theater. She was a little nervous, if she was honest. Too many weird things were happening, and none of them made sense. Despite the heat now blasting from her vents, she shivered. *I have a bad feeling about where all this is heading.*

8

As they drove through Turtle Cove to reach the theater, Kaylee was struck again by what an odd location the Cases had chosen for their theater. The area around the Main Street shops still had foot traffic, even on such a chilly day, but once they moved into the more run-down part of town near the warehouses, there were far fewer people around.

Are the Cases counting on word of mouth to bring an audience when the play opens? She supposed that would explain their eagerness to include people from the community. Each local in the cast would invite friends and family to be in the audience.

Still, there were several empty buildings closer to the bustle of the main streets. She pulled her car into the parking lot near the theater and stared up at the old factory. She thought of what Delia had said about the Cases' money concerns. *Maybe the ropewalk was simply a great bargain.*

Kaylee hopped out of her SUV as Reese was rooting around in the bed of his truck. "If I'm going off to do some handyman work, I should be ready to actually *do* it," he said as he pulled out his tool belt and buckled it around his waist.

"I appreciate this," Kaylee said.

Reese smiled. "Anything for a friend."

When they reached the entrance of the theater, Kaylee expected the door to be locked, but Reese hauled it open and waved Kaylee in ahead of him. In the lobby, Belinda was leaning against a table, flipping through papers on a clipboard. When she saw Kaylee and Reese, she straightened up and set the clipboard beside her. "This is a lovely surprise. What brings you two here today?"

"I was having lunch with Kaylee, and she talked me into reconsidering your offer to be the theater's handyman," Reese said. "At least part-time."

Belinda clapped her hands. "Wonderful." She beamed at Kaylee. "You're my hero again."

As she hadn't been expecting Reese to announce that the change was inspired by her, Kaylee didn't quite know what to say.

Thankfully Reese saved her from needing to say anything. "I brought my tools," he said, patting the belt. "In case you had anything that needs to be done right now."

"Actually, we do have a few little problems." Belinda laughed lightly. "I guess it's to be expected with such an extensive remodel. Rhett says we have growing pains."

"What sort of little problems?" Reese asked.

"Well, the faucet in the bathroom off the foyer is dripping. Plus, the security system flatly isn't working. It says it is, but it's not."

"I'll check on those things right now," Reese said. "Let me start with the wiring on the security system. It shouldn't be having any issues since it's so new."

Belinda raised both hands and shrugged. "Well, it is."

"I need to run to the truck for my voltage meter," Reese said, then left.

As the theater door swung shut behind Reese, Belinda turned to Kaylee. "Do you moonlight as the handyman's assistant, or did something else bring you out today? Not that I'm not glad to see you."

"I wanted to check on how Sullivan is doing," Kaylee said, not untruthfully. "He's been through a lot."

Belinda's eyes filled with tears, and she gave Kaylee a rather watery smile. "Sullivan is wonderful. He and Gilbert have been inseparable since Sullivan came home. You should have seen them when I left this morning, sharing Gilbert's bed. Those two never share anything, so that showed how much they missed each other. It was easily the sweetest thing I've ever seen." She reached out and took Kaylee's hands. "I'm so grateful to you for finding my dog."

"I can't take any of the credit for that. It was all Bear." Kaylee glanced around for signs of the Cases' dachshunds, but they weren't in the lobby. "The dogs aren't here today?"

Belinda shook her head. "They're still at the cottage. I wanted to give them a quiet day together. I think they both needed it, though I have to admit, it's hard for me to be here when they're alone at home. I don't think I'm going to be completely comfortable with Sullivan being out of my sight for a long time."

"At least the cottage isn't terribly far away," Kaylee said, recalling the street Mary had mentioned it was on. The house wasn't quite within an easy walk of the theater, but it would be doable on a pleasant day.

"Yes, I'm glad of that. If I crack under the strain, I can run home and check on them." Belinda's cheeks pinked slightly. "And I may have already done that once today."

"I don't blame you. I'd be a wreck if I had to leave Bear alone after just getting him back from something so scary."

"Speaking of which, where is the hero of the hour? I don't have any steak, but I could sneak him a bite of chicken salad."

Kaylee smiled but shook her head. "Bear doesn't need more treats. My assistant at The Flower Patch spoils him shamelessly. He's with her now."

"Well if I can't give him treats, maybe I'll drop by later with a new toy."

"He'll love you for life," Kaylee assured her. Belinda scooped up her clipboard, and Kaylee sensed she was about to end the conversation. Kaylee wasn't ready for that. "Tell me, are you still getting lilies every day?"

Belinda sighed and dropped the clipboard on the table. "There was another one on the stage this morning. That's part of the reason why I know the security system isn't working. No one was in the theater when I got here, but I found a fresh lily on the stage. It's not fun or charming anymore. It's creepy."

"I'm sure it is," Kaylee said.

"I threw the one this morning straight into the trash before Rhett could see it. They upset him even more than they do me." Belinda absently wiped her hands on her pants. "I think he's jealous, while I'm more freaked out."

"Would you mind if I take today's lily?" Kaylee asked.

Belinda's eyebrows lifted in surprise, but she said, "Sure, if you want it. I imagine it's wilted by now, though."

"Wilted isn't a problem. I want to compare it to a piece of plant found in the shed where Sullivan was held."

Belinda's eyes widened even more. "You think the flowers might be connected to the dognapping?" She peered around fearfully. "But the flower person seems to be able to come and go at will. What'll keep him from grabbing one of my dogs again?"

"I'm sure Reese will figure out what's wrong with the security system," Kaylee said gently. "That should put a stop to the flowers."

"For now." Belinda shivered though the theater lobby was warm. Then her eyes widened again. "The same security company that did the theater also did our cottage. What if someone tries to get the dogs from our house?"

"I'm sure that's not very likely," Kaylee said, though she had barely gotten through the sentence before Belinda was rushing through the theater doors.

Kaylee picked up the clipboard Belinda had discarded, more from curiosity than anything else. She wondered at all the small details that went into running a theater. The papers on the clipboard included notes about lighting cues and props, as well as a list of all the roles in the upcoming production and the actors who would play them.

She went through the actor list, smiling as she recognized names. DeeDee's girls were listed under the heading *Townspeople*. She also saw that Delia's name was highlighted with a question mark above it. Kaylee assumed that meant Belinda wasn't sure if Delia would be well enough for the role.

She saw other names she recognized, and mentally called up what she knew about each one. Quinn Selby was Belinda's niece, the girl whose eyes were so red from allergies and, quite possibly, from heartbreak. Kaylee made a mental note to ask Quinn herself about that. Mike Mortenson was the newest member of the troupe, and he made Delia uncomfortable. Kaylee tapped the page. There was something else she knew about him, something Belinda had said. She tried to call up the conversation in her memory, but came up dry. She'd think about it later.

Then she saw Elliot Wythe's name. Delia had seemed fond of the man, but clearly considered him a bit eccentric. He believed in ghosts, and specifically believed the theater was haunted. Kaylee wondered why. *Is it something he says about every theater, or did he experience something odd?* She decided that she needed to chat with Mr. Wythe.

She set the clipboard on the desk as Rhett trotted out the door to the auditorium. He stopped and glared around the foyer before focusing on Kaylee and walking her way. "Have you seen Belinda? I thought she was going to stay out here and sign for a delivery of some props from the mainland."

"She went home," Kaylee said. "She wanted to check on Sullivan."

Rhett walked over to the door, pushed it open and leaned out. "How long ago?"

"Not sure, maybe five minutes?"

"Has anyone come in since Belinda left?"

Kaylee shook her head. "I was here before she went, and I haven't seen anyone else."

His forehead creased as he frowned. "And you're here because . . . ?"

"I came with Reese. Mostly I wanted to see how Sullivan was doing."

Rhett's frown didn't ease. "He's fine. Did you scare Belinda into going home? There's no reason to get crazy over this. The dog is fine."

"She said someone has been getting into the theater despite your security system. She said your cottage had the same system. I think that's what worried her." *It didn't have anything to do with me, you grouch.*

Rhett crossed his arms over his chest. "You said you came in with Reese. Where is he?"

Kaylee was getting a little annoyed at the cross-examination, but she made an effort to answer pleasantly. "Checking the wiring of the security system."

Finally, Rhett bobbed his head. "I'm going to go outside and watch for the delivery. If Reese has anything to report on the system, I'll be out front."

"I'll let him know."

Once Rhett left, Kaylee decided to hunt for other members of the troupe who might be interested in talking. She'd pass along the message to Reese if she saw him. She crossed the lobby and pushed open one of the wide double doors leading into the main part of the theater. The audience lights were off, but the stage was illuminated. Several actors were gathered in the lit area.

Kaylee blinked, waiting for her eyes to adjust, then headed for the stage. The slope of the aisle made her feel a little off-kilter in the dark so she walked slowly and carefully.

One of the actors straightened up as Kaylee approached and called out loudly, "It is my lady. O, it is my love!"

Kaylee thought the line sounded vaguely familiar but couldn't place it immediately. She studied the actor who'd spoken the words. He was tall and quite thin, to the point of appearing almost gangly. He had snow-white hair and a neatly trimmed beard to match.

"She speaks yet she says nothing. What of that?" the man said, waving his hand theatrically in her direction. "Her eye discourses. I will answer it."

That was when Kaylee recognized the lines. "Aren't you a tiny bit . . . mature to play Romeo?"

"Perhaps a little," he said, dropping his hand. "Age is a cruel tyrant that imprisons a fiery youth in the walls of an old man."

"You must be Elliot Wythe," Kaylee guessed.

"I must." He bowed deeply. "I truly must."

"I heard you believe this theater is haunted."

"And you do not?" He raised white tufts of eyebrow. "How could a place with so much history avoid visits from those who have gone before?"

Kaylee pushed her hands into the pockets of the light jacket she wore. The theater was cooler than she would have preferred. "So this is more of a theoretical haunting? You haven't heard moaning or chains rattling?"

He lifted his chin with a haughty expression. "In my experience, dear lady, ghosts are subtle presences. They haunt with a lighter hand than old movies would have you believe."

Kaylee almost laughed at the man's overly dramatic wording, but she wasn't sure if he would take offense. "Is that right?" she asked, keeping her tone polite and serious.

"Flowers arrive on the stage with no hand to bring them through locked doors," Elliot went on. "And they are always lilies, the flower of the dead. Obviously it is a specter bringing them over from the great beyond."

"Or someone with a weird sense of humor playing a prank," Quinn said as she walked over and sat down on the edge of the stage. The young woman's eyes were less red than before, and she wasn't sniffling. "Elliot imagines things."

Elliot clutched his chest. "I am wounded by such a wild accusation. And you forget the specter leaves the stage door hanging open, even when everyone is sure the door is shut."

Quinn shook her head, sending her short ponytail swinging. "Maybe the door is hung crooked. Belinda says Rhett kept trying to cut corners on the renovations."

"Child, why must you cling to the mundane when the ethereal is at work?" Elliot asked. "Consider Delia. She was pushed, and everyone knows poltergeists are very pushy."

Quinn laughed. "So now we have a poltergeist?"

Elliot flourished one hand. "Perhaps."

"Why would a ghost push Delia?" Kaylee asked.

Elliot shrugged, a huge gesture that nearly put his shoulders against his ears. "I can only guess. We know this is not the ghost of a simple thespian, as the theater is too new. So it must be the spectral presence of some rowdy, violent man who once slaved away on these very docks. Perhaps his heart was broken in life by his lady love, so he is hostile toward women."

"So it's the ghost of a dock worker?" Kaylee suggested.

"Alas, I expect so," Elliot replied. "If we were in a proper theater, the ghost would be more dignified. We thespians are delicate of heart, but basically gentle souls and courtly of manner."

Quinn laughed again. "Right. Actors are all about dignity and courtly manners." She shook her head and hopped off the stage. "I'm going to go outside and get some fresh air. Try not to scare Kaylee off."

"I would never chase away so fair a maid," Elliot said, which made Quinn laugh again as she headed out the door.

"If it was a ghost that pushed Delia, how did Sullivan end up in a shed so far away?" Kaylee asked.

"I imagine the ghost left the stage door open and the little dog merely ran away when Delia fell. He was probably found by a good Samaritan who simply hadn't yet brought him home." He pointed at Kaylee. "You mark my words, we'll discover I am right. It's a ghost, I declare, and I am never wrong."

"Well, I appreciate you telling me about it," Kaylee said. "I need to find Reese now. Have you seen him? He's the handyman."

"I know young Reese," Elliot said. "He is a good sort. I think he's working backstage, though I cannot say where. I am a man of the spotlight, not the shadows."

"Of course." Kaylee started toward the steps leading to the stage, as she intended to access the backstage through the wings, but she'd barely gone two steps when the doors to the lobby burst open.

Quinn stumbled in, shrieking. "Someone help! Rhett has been run over!"

9

A near stampede of actors thundered past Kaylee, all heading up the aisle toward Quinn. Since no one had paused to call 911, Kaylee pulled out her phone and made the call, following the group as she did. She couldn't offer any details during the brief conversation, but she didn't want to wait any longer before getting help for Rhett.

When she disconnected the call and went outside, she found the actors crowded around Rhett, who sat perched on the edge of an empty planter box near the front of the theater. The right arm of his sweater was torn, and Rhett held a towel clamped over the part of his arm that showed through the hole. He was also dirty and rumpled.

Kaylee felt a rush of relief that he wasn't injured more seriously. "What happened?"

"Some crazy person tearing out of the parking lot," Rhett explained. "I jumped away, but I think one of the side mirrors hit my arm. It was all a little fast. I figure the driver didn't see me."

"Didn't see you?" Quinn asked, her voice still a little loud from stress. "Were you hunkered down between two parked cars? How could someone not see you in broad daylight in a sparsely used parking lot? And who was it? In this lot, we ought to know the person."

"Calm down, Quinn," Rhett said. "It was probably someone who pulled into the lot by mistake and wasn't paying proper attention. It only takes a momentary glance at a cell phone to cause an accident. Listen, it's no big deal. Nothing's broken. It's not much more than a scrape."

"You still ought to have it checked," Quinn said. "I'm driving you to the hospital."

"No, you're not," Rhett insisted. "I'm fine, and there's no reason to fuss."

"I'm afraid I've already fussed," Kaylee said. "I called 911 as soon as Quinn announced that you'd been run over. The ambulance is on its way, and you should have your arm professionally examined."

Rhett's expression darkened and he stood up, then swayed slightly on his feet and sank back down onto the planter's edge. "Fine. But I wish you hadn't called. If we get too many weird accidents connected with this theater, it could kill us. A new business can't survive a reputation for being dangerous, and this one has already gotten enough bad press."

"No one is going to blame the theater for this," Kaylee said.

His expression sharpened. "You think not? I'd expect better sense from a business owner. Why are you here again? Shouldn't you be focusing on your own business?"

Kaylee could tell she'd worn out her welcome with Rhett so she didn't push back. "You're right. I'll go tell Reese I'm leaving." *And along the way, I'll pick up a sample of today's lily from the trash backstage.*

Rhett didn't answer, though he mumbled something before giving his full attention to the blood seeping through the towel he held against his arm. Kaylee headed toward the theater and saw Mike Mortenson standing a short distance from the rest of the actors. He was watching Rhett closely, though he noticed when Kaylee approached him.

"Ma'am," he said in greeting, taking a half step backward as though he thought he might be in her way.

"Do you know if anyone actually saw the accident?" she asked.

He shrugged, making only brief eye contact with her. "Quinn

maybe, since she's the one who was screaming like a banshee over it. The rest of us were all inside."

Kaylee glanced behind her and located Quinn, who stood hovering over Rhett. Kaylee was fairly certain that Rhett wouldn't appreciate her walking back over there, so she'd have to talk to the girl later. She returned her gaze to Mike. "What do you think about the weird things that have been happening around here?" she asked. "Are you with Elliot on the ghost theory?"

Mike smiled slightly, then ducked his head again. "I'm not much for ghosts. As for weird stuff, weird and actors go together. I don't know that this bunch is much weirder than any other."

"I understand you joined the troupe recently," Kaylee said. "How has it been going?"

"It's all right. Everyone works hard, but I don't know about this theater. I'm no businessman, but it seems a bad choice, coming here and opening in November."

Kaylee tilted her head toward Rhett. "Do you think the Cases are good businesspeople?"

"I hope they are." Mike's attention sharpened as he gazed over her shoulder. "The ambulance is here. I should go see if Rhett wants anything."

"And I'd best move along before he notices I'm still here," Kaylee said.

Mike grinned at her then, and Kaylee was startled at the transformation to his face. He was quite handsome when he smiled. "Don't worry," he said. "Plenty of us prefer having you around." Then he ambled over to the rest of the crowd.

Kaylee considered for a moment whether she should stay outside, but she couldn't think of a single thing she could contribute, so she walked on into the lobby, then through to the theater. Though the spotlights were still on, no one was up on the stage or loitering nearby. Clearly Rhett's accident had sent everyone outside, which made Kaylee wonder how Reese had missed it. He must be hidden in the depths of the backstage area, unaware of the hullabaloo.

She climbed the steps to the stage and continued into the wings. In the darkness backstage, it took her quite a while to find the trash can where the wilted lily lay next to a collection of discarded coffee cups all displaying the Death by Chocolate logo. *Good to see everyone supports local business.*

Kaylee fished in her purse for a small evidence bag, which she'd taken to carrying for exactly this kind of situation. She used the tip of a pen to coax a bit of the lily into the bag, then sealed it and tucked it back into her purse.

She pulled out her phone and dialed Nick's cell phone. He answered on the first ring, his tone cheerful. "What can I do for my favorite florist?"

"I'm wondering what I might do for you," she said. "Or for the theater investigation. I collected a piece of lily at the theater. Whoever has been leaving them is still doing it. I want to compare the piece I got today with the one from the shed where Sullivan was kept."

Nick didn't answer right away, and Kaylee tried to be patient. Finally he said, "That should be fine, but I still don't know if the sheriff wants to pursue the dognapping, especially since Delia seems to have grown less sure that she was pushed."

That surprised Kaylee. *Why would she take back her original statement?* "What does she say happened?"

"She says she's not sure, not after being unconscious. She says she can't be certain what is a memory and what might be a dream."

"I see. Have you heard about Rhett?"

Another pause, then Nick's voice sounded unsure. "What about him?"

"Apparently he was hit by a car out in front of the theater," Kaylee said. "I called 911. An ambulance came. I'm surprised you didn't know."

"Yeah, so am I. I think I'll come over. Are you outside with the victim?"

"No. They didn't seem to need me out there." Kaylee shifted nervously. The dark recesses of the backstage could be more than a little ominous with no one else around.

"Okay, well, maybe I'll see you there. I'm on my way."

"Wait, what about the flower?" Kaylee asked. "Do you want me to compare it with the plant matter we found at the shed last night?"

"Oh, right. Let me check in on Rhett, and I'll meet you at Akin Funeral Chapel in about an hour. I should be free by then, since I'm clearly not a primary on the hit-and-run."

"Okay, I'll see you then." Kaylee hung up the phone and slipped it into her purse beside the scrap of lily. She often used the lab at the funeral home to compare plant samples, so she knew they'd have what she needed as long as Nick remembered to bring the piece he had.

Now it really was time to find Reese. She wanted to get his perspective on Rhett's accident.

She wandered down the dark hall that led toward the back door Rhett had shown her before. This time, she opened doors along the way, peeking into rooms in search of Reese. She was fascinated by the dressing rooms, with their rolling clothing racks and big mirrored vanities. They made her think of all the movies she'd seen where characters sat in front of mirrors dabbing on stage makeup. It was a different world from Kaylee's own academic background, and it had an aura of peculiar mystique.

She entered one of the dressing rooms and examined the makeup scattered across the table. Some of it was clearly new, but a couple of the makeup cases were battered, the contents well-used. Kaylee glanced into the different bags and was reminded that Mike was supposed to be particularly good with makeup. *What must it be like to be able to transform yourself into a totally different person?* She supposed that was what acting was all about—being someone you weren't.

"I think I'll stick with who I am." She turned away from the makeup table and reentered the hallway. She opened more doors and found a restroom, a supply closet, and a small office.

She slipped into the office and looked around. The room held two desks, and though they were small, they made the room feel crowded, especially with the tiny filing cabinet and two rolling chairs. As she turned to examine the poster on the wall next to one desk, her purse nudged the computer mouse and the monitor screen brightened, showing an image of Belinda and Rhett in some kind of period costumes. Kaylee wasn't going to poke around in the files on the computer, but she shifted her attention from the poster to the photo. The two actors appeared happy. The contrast with Rhett's usual demeanor made her think of how worried he seemed to be about the new theater. *I hope this story has a happy ending.*

On a whim, Kaylee scooted the mouse for the second computer. Though the screen brightened, it didn't display the computer's desktop. Instead, a password prompt popped up. *Why is one computer password-protected, but the other one isn't?* She supposed the computer with the password might hold all the financial records. It would make sense to have more security for those files.

What was she doing? Being nosy in the Cases' office wasn't helping her find Reese. She didn't want to end up late to meet Nick. However, at the exact moment that she decided to leave the office and continue her search for Reese, she spotted a dirty sheet of paper half-hidden in a pile. Though only a corner of the paper was showing, it caught her attention because it was discolored and shabby, as if it had spent some time outside. Kaylee gently tugged it out of the pile and held it up. The note appeared to have been crumpled up at one point and then smoothed out. The words on the page were scrawled and faded, not neatly printed like the fan note in Sullivan's saddlebag.

Time is running out.

"Time for what?" Kaylee whispered. She flipped the note over, searching for any possible clue. The paper seemed ordinary enough, if a bit heavier than the computer paper she usually handled. She looked from the desk in front of her to the other. Whose desk was this? Who had sent the note? Did Rhett or Belinda know what it was about? And was it connected to someone nearly running over Rhett?

She had plenty of questions and no good answers. She snapped a photo of the note with her phone, then carefully slid the paper back into the untidy pile and crept out of the office. The hallway was still empty. With a sigh, Kaylee started opening doors again. She found another dressing room, this one with a dressing table completely devoid of makeup or any other personal items. Clearly it wasn't being used for this production.

The next room was a prop closet crammed with all kinds of oddities: wooden chairs stacked on top of one another, a box of tobacco pipes and eyewear, a pile of telephones from various eras. She even saw what appeared to be a guillotine against the far wall with a large ax leaning against it. *That's not alarming at all.*

The final door led to a wardrobe closet. As packed as the prop room, it mainly contained metal racks full of clothes and shelves full of shoes lining the walls. Kaylee thought about how much fun it would be to try on some of the unusual costumes, as the colorful dresses and coats pulled on her fond memories of playing dress-up when she was a child. But she firmly closed the door behind her and stood in the hall.

She saw no more doors that she hadn't opened. That left her with one big question. *Where is Reese?* Then she smacked herself lightly in the head. She'd probably missed him. He'd almost certainly gone outside after checking on the security system and was likely caught up in the situation with Rhett. There was a good chance she'd find Nick and Reese together once she got outside. *I've got to stop seeing mysteries behind every closed door.*

After giving herself a stern talking-to, Kaylee headed up the hall, through the theater and out into the parking lot, where she assumed she'd see Reese. Instead, she saw Rhett arguing with the ambulance driver about whether he needed to go to the hospital for an X-ray. The crowd of actors had thinned a bit, and Kaylee saw the parking lot was emptier as well. She figured some of the actors were taking advantage of their release to go find something more interesting to do. She did see Reese's truck, but the handyman himself was nowhere in sight.

So where is he? And where is Nick? She'd expected to find both of them, but she'd found neither.

Kaylee pulled out her phone and messaged Reese. *Where are you?* As she sent it, she noticed the time and yelped. She had to get out to the funeral home. She sent a quick glance at the theater, worry twisting her stomach. "Wherever Reese is, he'll message back," she said firmly. "Stop fussing." *If only it were that easy. Where are you, Reese?*

Swallowing down her nerves, she headed for her car. She needed to go identify a flower and talk to Nick. *If I can't find Reese, Nick will.* She just hoped she didn't need to get the police involved.

10

As Kaylee pulled into Akin Funeral Chapel's parking lot, she was glad to see Nick's cruiser. *At least someone is where he belongs.* And that reminded her that she hadn't been where she belonged all day. Though she was eager to talk to Nick about Reese, she took a moment to call Mary again. *I've taken terrible advantage of our friendship today.*

Mary picked up quickly. "How goes the mystery solving?"

"It's only getting more confusing," Kaylee admitted. "I'm sorry for not being there already, but I need to examine some plant samples at the funeral home. Nick is here."

"Don't even worry about it. You're trying to make our community a safer place, and it's quiet at the shop today."

Kaylee sighed deeply. "You're a gem. I hate to ask for one more favor, but if you need to go home and I'm not there yet, could you take Bear with you? I'll pick him up at your house."

"I'd be glad to, though I doubt that's going to happen," Mary said. "I was actually planning to stay after closing if it's all right with you. I desperately need to track down a Christmas present for Herb. He's a big kid over presents and always seems to figure out what I'm doing. So do you mind if I use the computer at the shop?"

"Of course you can," Kaylee said, feeling marginally better with a little of the guilt lifted. "Stay as long as you want. I promise to get there when I can."

"You sound stressed. Is there more that you haven't said?"

"A bit." Kaylee sighed. "I couldn't find Reese at the theater before I left, and it worries me. I searched everywhere."

"There are a lot of nooks and crannies at a theater, places you can't even find if you don't know they're there. He's probably tucked into one of those working on wiring or some such."

"It's bothering me that he vanished," Kaylee said. "And his truck is still in the theater lot."

"I still think you could be worrying about nothing," Mary said. "Reese is a strong guy. No one has run off with him. He was probably just somewhere in the theater. Herb and I once went to a play in an old theater in Seattle. Herb's cousin was in the play and he gave us a tour of the theater. It was like a rabbit warren with all the doors and twisting hallways. Plus, everywhere is so dark."

"It *was* awfully dark," Kaylee admitted.

"See?"

"But he didn't answer my text."

"Cell service is notoriously bad at some spots on the waterfront with all the interference," Mary said. "I expect you'll get an answer as soon as Reese is done with his project and in a better location. He's probably texting you and wondering why *you* haven't answered. You'll see—it'll prove to be a mix-up. Now, is Reese the only thing worrying you?"

"It's the main thing. There is a bit more, but I need to get inside and talk to Nick. I promise to catch you up when I see you."

"I'll hold you to that." Mary chuckled, then said goodbye and disconnected the call.

Kaylee tucked her phone away and started toward the building. Akin Funeral Chapel's high, sharply peaked roof gave it the appearance of an old church, a shape reflected again in the tall mullioned windows. Pale brick added to the trim, clean style.

As she entered the building and waited for her eyes to adjust to the softer lighting inside, Kaylee heard a voice she recognized. "Hello, Kaylee." It was Jay Akin, the twentysomething son of

Giles, who was the funeral home director and local coroner. "The deputy is waiting for you. I'll take you back," Jay said. He asked about the weather as they walked, and Kaylee managed not to chafe at the small talk when she was in a hurry to return to the theater and find Reese.

Jay left her at the door to the lab. She entered to see Nick slowly spinning on a stool. He hopped up as soon as Kaylee came in, but the brief sight of him playing with the stool amused her and softened some of the dread settling in her stomach. "You brought the flower?" she asked.

"Wouldn't be much point in coming otherwise." He waved toward the microscope. "It's over there."

Kaylee retrieved the second piece of lily from her purse as she walked across the room. "This shouldn't take long."

"Why? Are you in a hurry?" Nick asked as he joined her at the microscope.

"Yes, but we'll go into that after I examine these flowers." She prepped the slides, taking extra care so that her worry about Reese didn't translate into a mistake. Then she studied each slide, taking notes and measurements. When she finished, she glanced up at Nick. "Both of these are samples from a *Lilium auratum*. I'm certain."

Nick pointed at the slides. "I'm afraid *Lilium-whatever* doesn't mean much to me. Is it an unusual flower? Is it something you sell at The Flower Patch? Could someone be growing it on the island?"

"I don't believe anyone would be growing *Lilium auratum* here on the island," she said. "They're expensive and tough to get, even if you go through a wholesaler on the mainland. They're huge and not that popular. If I did use them, I'd have to special order them, and they'd probably be shipped in from Asia."

"So whoever is leaving these had to go to some trouble to get them? Maybe Simmons Kind of Wonderful in Eastsound sold them."

"Maybe. I would be surprised, but it's not impossible if the person was willing to pay for a special order. I went to that pet store in Eastsound and found that they sell the exact same pet bowls that we found in the shed. Gwen Simmons' storefront isn't terribly far from Pet Project. If the person who took Sullivan is the same as the one leaving the flowers, that person may have been flower shopping in Eastsound as well."

"Sounds as if I should probably talk to Gwen Simmons," Nick said.

"I could call her," Kaylee answered, remembering that she'd meant to stop by when she was in Eastsound, but then had been distracted by running into Reese. She felt a bit guilty since she'd promised Rhett that she'd look into it.

Nick shook his head. "Let me do it. I'm thinking more and more that I should keep this investigation official. It's getting complicated."

"Whatever you want to do." Kaylee snuck a glance at the clock on the wall. She hadn't been gone from the theater long, but she felt an increasing need to go find Reese. She tried not to be controlled by hunches and bad feelings, but too many weird things were going on with the theater, and she'd feel a lot better if she could talk to Reese.

"Okay, what's with you?" Nick asked. "You're practically jumping out of your skin."

"It's Reese," Kaylee said as she began cleaning up the microscope area, mostly to keep her hands busy and possibly distract the extremely observant deputy. She didn't want him thinking her concern for Reese was more than what she would feel for any of her good friends—she already got more than enough teasing about her love life. "He was at the theater earlier, checking the wiring for the security system. Belinda said it's not working properly." Kaylee hesitated, suddenly wishing she'd asked more about that. "Before I came over here, I went hunting for him. He'd only gone with me to the theater so I wouldn't be there alone, so I wanted to let him know I was leaving. I searched all over. His truck was still in the lot, but he was nowhere to be found."

"Did you try calling him?" Nick asked.

"No," Kaylee admitted, feeling a little foolish. "I only texted him."

Nick pulled out his phone and tried a call. Kaylee held her breath, hoping that Reese would pick up. It wasn't long before Nick shook his head and stuffed his phone in his pocket. "We need to get to the theater and find him. Right now."

Kaylee waited while Nick gathered up the floral evidence, grateful that he was taking her concern seriously. She had something else she needed to tell him. "You know how I told you I searched all over the theater?"

Nick carefully slipped a slide into an evidence envelope. "Yeah?"

"I opened every door and went into every room. There was no one else backstage at the theater because everyone was outside with Rhett."

He paused and peered at her as what she said sank in.

She kept going. "One of the rooms I went into was an office. I assume it was Belinda and Rhett's office. And I looked around a little while I was there."

Nick folded his arms over his chest. "How little?"

"All right, it was quite a bit," she said. "I saw a pile of papers, and one of the papers sticking out of the pile looked weird. Dirty and wrinkled."

"Let me guess—you couldn't resist pulling it out."

"I guess not. It was a note. It wasn't signed, and it wasn't written in the same block letters used in the note from Sullivan's saddlebag, but it was ominous. It said, 'Time is running out.'"

"Time for what?" Nick asked.

"Your guess is as good as mine. But the note had been crumpled up at some point, and maybe even thrown in the trash. It was pretty dirty." Then she remembered and pulled out her phone. "I took a picture." She showed him the photo she'd snapped, and Nick squinted at the small screen for a moment.

"Send that to me," he said. "I want to look at it later and possibly chat with the Cases about it."

Kaylee winced. "Do you have to tell them how you got it?"

"I'll avoid mentioning your insatiable curiosity if I can." Now Nick's gaze darted to the clock. "In the meanwhile, we need to get going. I now have two reasons to get to the theater."

Nick swatted at the light switch as they left the lab, and Kaylee followed him down the hall. They waved at Jay as they passed his office but didn't stop to talk on their way out. Kaylee could tell Nick was just as alarmed by Reese's disappearance as she was.

"Do you want to ride with me?" Nick asked as they reached the parking lot. "I can bring you back for your car later."

"No, I need to get to the shop after we find Reese."

Her voice must have reflected how worried she felt, because Nick gave her a reassuring look. "Reese can take care of himself. We're going to go find out what he's been up to, and then I'll chew him out for scaring you."

"Thanks." Kaylee managed a smile that fell from her lips as soon as she turned to head for her SUV. As she slipped into the driver's seat, she issued a prayer for Reese's safety. "Please let us find him," she whispered. "And let him be okay."

11

Kaylee's fingers clenched the steering wheel so hard that her knuckles whitened as she followed Nick closely all the way to the theater. With her nerves strung so tight, she was especially glad of the lack of tourist traffic on the road. She tried telling herself that Reese was fine, but she wasn't buying it.

As they pulled into the lot, Kaylee saw that the small crowd was completely gone. For a moment, she wondered if Rhett had given in and gone to the hospital. Then she spotted two men talking near the doors. Rhett stood leaning against one of the wooden posts that held up the awning over the door, and next to him was Reese. As soon as her car was in park, Kaylee flung open her door and leaped out.

While she was jogging toward the two men, she heard Nick behind her. "You're in so much trouble, buddy," the deputy called.

Kaylee saw Rhett's eyes widen in alarm, but she barely registered that because of her relief at seeing Reese. "I hunted all over for you," she said, "but then I had to leave to identify some plant matter for Nick. Are you all right?"

Reese's welcoming smile slipped into an expression of concern. "I worried you? I'm sorry. I tried to call to find out where you were, but my phone is dead." He winced. "I guess I forgot to charge it last night."

"That's all right," Kaylee said, still feeling a little shaken with relief. "I know it was silly, but it freaked me out a little when I couldn't find you."

Reese rested his hands on his tool belt. "I was probably in the furnace room tracing the wiring."

"The furnace room door isn't easy to see," Rhett cut in. "We didn't want people wandering in there thinking it was a restroom or a dressing room, so it's tucked into a corner and painted to blend in with the wall."

"Well, after an inadvertent test run, I can vouch for the effectiveness of the camouflage." Kaylee realized she'd been clutching her purse and made a concerted effort to relax. "So did you figure out what was wrong with the security system?"

"Yeah, someone tampered with it." Reese addressed his next comment to Nick. "Part of it had been rewired to avoid tripping the alarm when the stage door is opened. I imagine that's how someone has been leaving the flowers."

Rhett narrowed his eyes. "That explains how someone left the flowers without the alarm going off, but it doesn't explain how someone has been able to open a locked door. We keep the stage door locked to anyone coming in from outside. Sometimes it might be unlocked while we're rehearsing, but we don't leave it that way overnight."

"Unless someone has been doing it intentionally," Nick said as he pulled out his notebook. "Tell me, could the rewiring have been done from outside?"

Reese shook his head. "It would be possible to rewire it from the outside, but not without cutting into the structure of the building to access the wires near the door. And that's not how this was done. I found the spot where it happened, and whoever did it was inside."

Nick frowned. "And you fixed it?"

Reese shrugged. "That's my job."

"It would have been nice to see it before you fixed it," the deputy said. "And I could have dusted for fingerprints."

"I took pictures," Reese dug his phone out of his pocket, then grimaced. "And I'll show them to you when I get a charge."

"Text them to me as soon as you can," Nick said. "And if you'll show me the location, that would be great." He faced Rhett. "Do you have any idea when someone could have rewired the security system?"

"It might have happened the day of the auditions," Rhett answered. "We had dozens of people coming and going. No one would have noticed one more."

"There were a lot of people there," Kaylee agreed, "but weren't you getting flowers before then?"

"That morning, but not before that," Rhett said. "And the person could have come in after we first arrived. It was a while before either Belinda or I walked out to the stage and saw the flower."

"So probably the day of the audition," Nick said, scribbling on his notepad. "Do you have a list of everyone who tried out?"

Rhett nodded. "They signed in. Belinda should have the list in the office. And the rest of the troupe was here."

"I saw someone," Kaylee said tentatively. "Someone who wasn't a member of the troupe. He wore all black, and I assumed he was a stagehand. But Delia told me you hadn't hired any yet."

Nick perked up at that, his pen poised over the pad. "I remember you telling me about him. I haven't been able to find the guy."

"Delia was right," Rhett said. "We don't have any stagehands yet. They'll be coming over from the mainland eventually, but for these early days, we're using members of the troupe to do some of the stagehand activity. It's a cost-saving measure."

"Then it was a member of the troupe," Kaylee surmised. "It wasn't Mike or Elliot though. I've talked to both of them, and the guy didn't look like either one."

"Can you describe him?" Nick asked.

Kaylee pulled up her recollection of the moment. "He was

about medium height, fairly average, really. He was wearing a black knit hat. He didn't have any facial hair." Then she suddenly had a flash of memory of a pale streak on the man's face. "A scar. I think he had a scar on his cheek." She indicated where on her own face. "Right there."

Rhett cleared his throat. "We don't have anyone in the troupe with a scarred face. Whoever that was, he didn't belong backstage."

Kaylee couldn't help but notice the pallor that Rhett had developed at her description. He knew who she was talking about. She could tell Nick caught the change in the man as well.

Nick narrowed his eyes at Rhett. "Do you know anyone who might fit that description?"

Rhett tightened his jaw. "We've barely met anyone outside of the auditions and the work done on the remodel. Our decision to move to Turtle Cove wasn't made based on either of us knowing anyone here, and since we arrived, we haven't exactly had time to be social."

Kaylee noticed that wasn't exactly an answer to Nick's question. "Maybe it was someone from the mainland," she suggested. "We may be an island, but we're not hard to reach."

"Why would someone come out from the mainland?" Rhett demanded.

"That's what we're trying to determine," Nick answered mildly, as if he didn't notice the dark red filling Rhett's face.

"Could the man I saw have been the person driving the car that nearly hit you?" Kaylee asked Rhett.

Rhett shot a fierce glare in her direction.

"Mr. Case, your previous answers to my questions about the car and driver were extremely vague," Nick said, speaking before Rhett could answer. Rhett pulled his attention away from Kaylee and gazed at the deputy, who continued speaking. "I hoped you'd have more details now that the shock has subsided.

Even if you don't want to press charges, I would like to find the person and impress upon him or her the importance of careful driving here in Turtle Cove."

"No, I don't have any more details. It happened very fast, and it was nothing," Rhett snapped. "Someone being inattentive. It happens all the time. I didn't see the driver. I was busy trying not to get run over."

"What can you tell me about the vehicle?" Nick asked.

"It was a car and it was moving." Rhett had clearly come to the end of his patience. "Look, I don't need police involvement here. No harm was done. I expect it scared the guy as much as it did me."

"Guy?" Nick echoed. "You saw it was a man?"

"It's a generic word." Rhett rolled his eyes. "I don't actually know if it was a man or a woman. Whoever it was just kept moving."

"So apparently it didn't scare *him* enough to stop," Nick observed.

"Yeah, apparently not. Now, I have rehearsals to deal with. If you'll excuse me, I'm done wasting my time here."

"Rehearsals?" Kaylee asked. "From the emptiness of this parking lot, I thought everyone had gone home. Is Belinda here?" She wouldn't mind asking Belinda about the note she'd seen. Somehow she thought the actress would be more forgiving of her reading the note than Rhett would be.

Rhett shook his head. "I'm going to work around her absence. The others will be returning any time now. I still need to finalize some blocking and lighting, and any warm body will do for that. Belinda wanted to spend the rest of the day with Sullivan. His disappearance was very hard on her, on all of us. Now I must ask you *all* to leave."

"Before I go," Reese said, speaking up for the first time in a while, "I need to know if you want me to reset the security system."

"And I want to see the location of the tampering," Nick said.

"No," Rhett said firmly to the deputy. "I want to drop this." Then he waved a hand at Reese. "But you can reset the system. Do that and go. You can bill me for the work."

Nick held up a hand. "If someone has been breaking in, maybe I should take a look before you eliminate the evidence."

"Not necessary," Rhett said. "Reese will fix it, and we'll forget about it. It's some nutty fan leaving flowers, not a federal offense."

"You're taking all this very lightly," Nick pressed. "Does your wife feel the same way? She seemed quite shaken by the note we found in your dog's saddlebag. If someone is leaving threatening notes, I want to nip this in the bud. These things can escalate."

"The note wasn't threatening," Rhett insisted.

"Was that the only note?" Nick asked.

"Of course." Rhett sounded exasperated. "You're all overreacting."

Kaylee bubbled with frustration at the man's stonewalling. "How can it be overreacting when one of the members of your theater troupe ended up in the hospital after an attack?"

"She may have imagined the push," Rhett said. "Or she could have made it up so Belinda wouldn't be mad at her for letting Sullivan run off."

"You could have ended up in the hospital with her," Kaylee said. "No one imagined the car that nearly ran you down."

Rhett blew up. "All of you out! Just go! I have work to do. I don't have time for conspiracy theories. What is wrong with the people on this island?"

He shoved past Kaylee and into the theater. As Kaylee stepped out of the red-faced man's path, she mused that the people of Turtle Cove weren't the ones acting crazy. Rhett seemed almost afraid of Nick investigating the strange happenings at the theater.

Nick grinned at Reese and Kaylee. "We certainly worked

him up. Makes you wonder, doesn't it?"

Reese continued to stare at the theater door as it swung shut behind Rhett. "It really does."

Nick wished them a good evening and left, which reminded Kaylee of how much she'd taken advantage of Mary. "I have to go," she said to Reese. "Poor Mary has had to hold down the fort alone all day."

"Do you want me to walk you to your car?" Reese asked.

Kaylee smiled, appreciating the gesture. "No, I'll be fine. Sounds like you have work to do."

"Yes, I'd better go reset the security system so I can get out of here." He placed a gentle hand on her arm. "I'm truly sorry for scaring you today."

"That's all right. I'm glad you're okay." She hesitated, then added, "When you get home, could you text me? I know I'm being silly, but I have some residual anxiety going."

"I'll text you as soon as I've plugged it in long enough to turn it on."

"Okay." Kaylee gazed up at the theater. The outside lights were dark, and the hulking shadow of the building was ominous in the gathering darkness. She shuddered as a sense of foreboding swept over her. It had been a hard day, and Kaylee had the feeling her troubles were nowhere near over.

12

Kaylee pulled into a parking space in front of The Flower Patch. Though it was slightly past closing time, light still shone from the windows, so Kaylee knew Mary hadn't left with Bear. She saw that Death by Chocolate was also blazing with light, and decided to pop in and grab a treat for Mary to take home.

As soon as she stepped through the door, Jessica rushed around the counter to give her a hug. "Thank goodness you're here. I've been desperate all day."

"What happened?" Kaylee asked, worry washing over her for the umpteenth time that day.

"Oliver dropped a leaf this morning!"

Jessica's panic over her beloved geranium made Kaylee smile. Jessica was convinced that Oliver was so sensitive to the world around him that he could predict coming catastrophe.

Kaylee glanced toward the plant, which appeared healthy and well, as always. "I'm sorry you've had a stressful day, but if it helps, Oliver seems fine."

"You think?" Jessica peered at the geranium for a moment, then turned her scrutinizing gaze on Kaylee. "How has your day been? You look tired."

"My day's been up and down. I lost Reese for a while, though that turned out to be a simple case of not charging a phone. And Rhett Case was nearly run over, though he's apparently fine, if a little grouchy. And I found out the lily discovered with Belinda's dog is the same species as the ones being left at the theater."

Jessica nodded sagely. "I heard about the dog being located. That must have been such a relief for the Cases."

"That's for sure," Kaylee said. She nodded toward the pastry case. "Can I get some treats for Mary? I've left her at the shop all day by herself, and I want to give her something nice to take home."

"I have some of that pumpkin fudge she and Herb love. I only carry it this time of year, and this batch has mini chocolate chips in it."

"That sounds perfect. Can you make up a box for me, please?"

"Of course, but don't think you're going to get away too easy. I'm sure I haven't heard everything." Jessica walked behind the counter and began folding a small box for the fudge.

"I don't know that I have anything more interesting to tell you," Kaylee said glumly. She really hadn't learned much for all her running around today. "Oh, I found out that the stranger I saw backstage at the auditions wasn't a stagehand because they haven't hired any. I do think Rhett recognized my description of the man, though. He turned white as a sheet."

Jessica plucked squares of fudge from a tray with waxed paper and placed them in the box. "What did the not-a-stagehand look like?"

Kaylee repeated the description she'd given at the theater. "Medium height and no facial hair, but I think he had a scar on his cheek."

Jessica froze and traced a line on her cheek with her finger. "Right here?"

Kaylee's senses tingled. "You've seen him?"

Jessica continued to gaze at her wide-eyed as she nodded. "He's been in here. We don't get nearly as many non-islanders right now, so strangers stand out more. And I definitely remember the scar."

"Anything else you recall?"

Jessica nodded again. "I remember thinking how much first impressions can be deceiving. He's kind of mild-mannered, so at first you might think he's a bit of a pushover. But one day when he came in, I overbalanced while I was sitting on a stool, and the guy caught my arm to keep me from falling. That's when I realized he was solid muscle. I bet he could bench press both of us."

"So he's been in here more than once," Kaylee surmised.

"Yeah, he's a regular now. Comes in every day, but at odd hours." Jessica hugged herself, and her gaze swept the shop as if she thought he might be lurking in there as she spoke. "He comes in within minutes of my unlocking the door in the morning or just before I close up in the evening. He's always the only one here when he arrives, and it's always before Gretchen comes in or after she leaves. I figured he worked odd hours, but now I'm completely spooked." She held out an arm to show Kaylee her goose bumps.

"Nick needs to hear this, and he might have some advice for you. In fact, he'll probably come over."

Jessica pressed her lips together into a thin line as she tucked in the lid on the box of fudge. "I'll call, but I don't know what to do. We have extended hours tonight, but now I'm uneasy. I especially hate the idea of being alone here after the flower shop is closed."

"Let me take this to Mary," Kaylee said, holding up the box, "and then I'll come and stay with you until closing if you want."

"I hate to ask you to do that," Jessica said, but Kaylee could see the hope and relief in her eyes.

"I insist. I'll be right back."

The *Closed* sign hung on the door of The Flower Patch, and the lights closest to the doors were out. For a moment, Kaylee worried that Mary had left while she was next door talking with Jessica, but when she let herself in with her key, she heard a chorus of welcoming barks from Bear and the scuttle of his toenails on the wood stairs as he raced down from the second floor to greet her. Mary followed more sedately in his wake.

"I'm sorry for keeping you here so late," Kaylee said as she offered the box of fudge. "I brought you a treat to make up for it a little."

"You don't need to make up for anything. But I'm not going to pass up one of Jessica's treats." Mary took the box then waved toward the stairs that led to the second-floor office. "I'm still on the computer. I didn't realize the fishing lures Herb put on his list were going to be so obscure. It's a good thing I started searching early, since some of them are custom-made."

"Does that mean you need a little more time?" Kaylee asked hopefully.

Mary was peeking into the box, but she looked up at Kaylee's question. "A little, if you don't mind. I'm actually in the middle of bidding on an online auction for a vintage reel that's on the list too."

"Take all the time you need. It works out well, actually." She quickly explained about Jessica and the fake stagehand. "I promised I'd stay with her until Nick arrived. It shouldn't be long."

"Go on." Mary flapped her hands at Kaylee in a shooing motion. "I'll stay with Bear."

Kaylee gave her a quick hug. She was blessed by how supportive Mary had been all day, but she knew her friend must be ready to get home to her husband. "If Nick does show up, and I feel certain he will, I'll come right back and let you go."

"No hurry," Mary said. "I've got time."

Bear gave Kaylee a distinctly reproachful stare when he saw her moving toward the front door again. When she kept walking, he added a sharp bark. "I know, Bear," Kaylee said in an appeasing tone. "We'll go for a nice walk in a little bit, I promise."

Mary scooped him up. "Don't let him fool you. He's had a perfectly nice day with walks and treats, not to mention dinner. I'm glad you keep some of his food here."

Bear's dark eyes followed Kaylee out the door, making her

feel guilty. Still, seeing the relief on Jessica's face when she walked back into Death by Chocolate eased a good bit of her remorse.

"Mary doesn't mind you staying with me?" Jessica asked hopefully. "Nick said he's on his way, but he had to do something first. He didn't specify what, so I don't know how long it might take."

"Mary said she doesn't mind a bit," Kaylee said. "She's trying to track down some Christmas gifts for Herb on the computer."

"Online shopping is so convenient." Jessica bent to get a cloth from under the counter and began wiping down the small tables where people enjoyed their coffee and chocolate treats. "I try to buy as much as possible from local vendors, but sometimes you need the convenience and selection that the Internet offers."

Kaylee suspected the change of subject was intentional to distract Jessica from her worry over the stranger, so she played along. "It's so true." Kaylee took a seat at one of the tables, suddenly aware of how tired she felt. It had been a very full day. "I do most of my shopping for my mainland friends and family here. Our little shops offer things you can't get anywhere else."

Jessica paused in her wiping. "Do you want a cup of coffee? I have a pot of decaf with a hint of chocolate."

"That sounds heavenly, thanks."

Jessica carried the cloth with her as she went to get two cups of coffee. Kaylee took the moment to enjoy the bakery, breathing in the scents of chocolate and spice that hung in the air. It was a comforting smell after her long day.

Jessica returned with two steaming mugs and took a seat across from Kaylee. "I decided we deserved real mugs instead of to-go cups. There's something about a real mug that feels homey, and I can use that feeling."

"I'm sorry you're so stressed, Jess," Kaylee said.

Jessica released a long exhale. "I'm calming down. I think

I overreacted to what you said earlier. The man who has been coming in here is always perfectly nice."

Kaylee took a long sip of the coffee, enjoying the warmth spreading through her. She hadn't realized how chilled she felt. She expected some of that was from going back and forth between shops and all the time she'd spent outside all day in the cold weather, but some was surely psychological as well. "This is delicious," she said finally. "As for the man, he may *be* perfectly nice. At this point, I don't know anything for sure."

"I'll still feel better when Nick gets here."

As if granting Jessica's wish, the door to the bakery opened and Nick walked in. His gaze scanned the room and zeroed in on Kaylee and Jessica.

Jessica stood. "Thanks for coming."

"Sure. You said it had something to do with Kaylee's mystery stagehand?" Nick gestured at the mugs of coffee. "And is there any way I could get one of those? I'm about frozen through. I had to stop and check on Mrs. Wolman after I left the theater. She heard a prowler."

"Oh no," Kaylee said, her spine tingling.

Nick shook his head. "Don't worry. I'm pretty sure it was a raccoon trying to get something to eat before winter settles in completely. Her trash can was knocked over. I picked it up for her since she's eighty if she's a day, and I didn't want her to have to stand out in the cold and do it."

"You're a true public servant," Jessica said. "Let me get you coffee."

Nick slipped into the chair next to Kaylee as Jessica hurried off. "I assume you're connected to her stagehand report," he said.

Kaylee nodded. "When I described him to her, she recognized him. Apparently he's a regular, which freaked her out a bit."

"Understandable, though we can't say for sure that the guy

you saw was doing anything nefarious. He could have come for the audition and simply had unfortunate fashion sense."

"I know," Kaylee admitted, as Jessica returned with another mug of coffee. "I do feel that it's more than that, but I could be wrong."

Nick grinned at her. "It does happen, if only occasionally."

Jessica set a mug on the table in front of the deputy. "I have to admit, I'm glad you're here. If you could stay while I lock up, I'd appreciate it. I'll close when we're done chatting. Any late owls in search of chocolate may be out of luck for tonight."

Nick took a long sip of his coffee, then pulled out his notepad. "Okay, I'm ready."

"On that note," Kaylee said, standing. "If no one needs me, I should get back and let Mary go home."

Jessica reached out and squeezed Kaylee's hand. "Thanks for staying with me."

"You're welcome." Kaylee smiled reassuringly at Jessica, then addressed Nick. "So, are we good?"

"As far as I know. If what Jessica tells me leads to more questions for you, I know where to find you."

When Kaylee walked next door to her shop, she was surprised to see Mary standing at the door, ready to let her in.

"Perfect timing," Mary said. "I won the auction, and I'm ready to go. I've straightened up already, so all you need to do is collect Bear. I think we're ready for tomorrow."

"No orders to fill?" Kaylee asked.

Mary shook her head. "Not for tomorrow. I did take a couple orders for Thanksgiving centerpieces, but it's too early to make them. I put in a wholesale order for the chrysanthemums, berries, and seedpods we need for them, though."

"You're a wonder." Kaylee flashed a grateful smile. "Now go, before Herb refuses to ever speak to me again."

"You don't have to worry about that. We're all Kaylee fans at my house." Mary walked behind the counter and gathered her purse and coat. Kaylee helped her into it, then locked the door behind Mary once she'd gone out.

Bear sat at Kaylee's feet, staring up at her expectantly. She leaned over and scratched his ears. "I'm sorry I've left you all day."

Bear wagged his tail and leaned into the petting, making it clear that her transgressions were forgiven.

"I promised you a walk," Kaylee said.

He danced around her feet as she snapped the leash on him, then he trotted along beside her with his head high and his tail waving like a metronome as they headed for the back door.

The area behind the shop held her trash cans and a small patch of grass, and it was poorly lit. She had a single sconce by the door, but it was far from bright, and Bear quickly tugged her out of its small pool of light.

Though Kaylee was eager to head for home, she didn't have the heart to rush Bear after being away from him for so long. He seemed intent on sniffing every blade of grass in the small patch while Kaylee waited, shivering a little as the cold sank into her.

Bear tugged her a little farther from the door. "Not that I am trying to hurry you along," Kaylee said, "but one of us is not wearing a fur coat. Aren't you cold?"

Bear sniffed a stick, clearly still in no hurry.

"This is retribution, right?" Kaylee asked as she drew her jacket tighter around herself. "You're getting me back for leaving you behind."

Bear glanced up at her, his mouth open and tongue lolling in a doggy grin, then returned to sniffing the same stick. Kaylee groaned.

She had just about decided to pick up the little dog and head home when Bear suddenly stopped sniffing and peered into the inky black night, growling deep in his chest.

"What is it?" Kaylee asked.

Bear took a few stiff-legged steps closer to the deep darkness between Death by Chocolate and The Flower Patch. "Is someone there?" *Please let it be the raccoon from Mrs. Wolman's.*

Then she saw something moving in the shadows, something far too big to be a raccoon.

"Nick?" Kaylee called as her heartbeat pounded in her ears. She knew it wasn't Nick. Bear would never growl at his favorite deputy that way.

A man emerged from the shadows and Kaylee's blood ran cold. It was the stagehand who wasn't.

13

Kaylee stood frozen in shock and fear as the man took one more step toward her. Bear strained against his leash, growling. "If you come one step closer," Kaylee said, proud that her voice barely shook, "I will scream. There is an Orcas Island sheriff's deputy right next door."

"I know." The man spoke so softly that Kaylee almost had to strain to hear over Bear's continued growling. "I came to offer you some advice. It would be in your best interest to stay out of things at the theater."

Kaylee stiffened. "And if I don't?"

The man offered her a cold smile. "I hope you don't make that choice. I'd hate to see anything happen to you. Or your little dog."

Kaylee gasped as the man focused on Bear. The dachshund lunged at the end of his leash and began barking fiercely. Kaylee took a deep breath and screamed Nick's name as loudly as she could—and quite loud it was.

The man melted into the shadows, slowly, as if to show he had no need to hurry. Kaylee hated how calm the man was, how sure of himself. She screamed again, this time not worrying about whether her words were intelligible and going strictly for volume. Bear continued to bark and tug at the leash as if to pull away and run the man down himself.

Nick burst from the back door of Death by Chocolate, Jessica on his heels. "That guy was here!" Kaylee shouted. "He threatened me. He went that way." She pointed, and Nick sprinted away.

Jessica rushed over to join Kaylee. "Are you all right?"

"I'm fine," Kaylee whispered, though fear still clawed at

her insides. Beside her, Jessica hunched and shivered in the icy chill. She wasn't dressed for the cold. "We should go inside. I need some tea."

Jessica nodded. They made their way into The Flower Patch's kitchen, where Kaylee put the kettle on the stove top. Kaylee intended to go home as soon as Nick brought the man through the door in cuffs, so Bear was still on his leash though no one was holding it. The little dog was perfectly at ease, and Kaylee relaxed a little in the light of Bear's normalcy.

"What did the guy say?" Jessica asked, her voice shaky, either from fear or the cold.

"He told me to stay out of things at the theater, or else something might happen to Bear or me," Kaylee said, never pausing in the comforting routine of fixing tea. She had to keep moving or she'd fall apart.

Perching on one of the kitchen chairs, Jessica wrapped her arms around herself. "That man was in my shop almost daily. I had no idea he was dangerous!"

"He had no reason to hurt you," Kaylee said. And she sincerely hoped he still didn't. "Now that he's shown himself in such a threatening way and attracted police attention, I rather doubt he'll be casually shopping anymore. If he does come by, you'll know what to do."

"You bet," Jessica said. "I'll lock myself and Oliver in my office and push furniture in front of the door while calling Nick."

Kaylee was glad to see some of Jessica's natural ebullience returning, though they both jumped when the kettle whistled behind her. Before she could pour, Nick came into the room. He was rumpled and clearly not happy.

"He got away," the deputy said, sounding winded. "I thought I was fast, but that guy runs like a rabbit."

"He did not remind me of a rabbit when he was standing

in the dark threatening me and Bear," Kaylee said. "More like a weasel."

Nick pulled his notebook out of his pocket. "Tell me his exact words if you can remember them."

Kaylee did. After filling Nick in, she asked him if he wanted a cup of tea to warm up. "I was about to pour for Jessica and me."

Nick shook his head. "I should get going and write this up. How about I walk each of you through locking up and then see you to your vehicles? If you don't mind passing on the tea."

"I don't mind," Jessica said. "I'll be happy to head home. I'll feel better when I'm safe and sound with Luke."

Kaylee felt a pang of jealousy, though only a small one. *It must be nice to have someone waiting at home who can be counted on to protect you.* As that thought flitted through her head, Bear leaned against her ankle, and Kaylee almost laughed as she looked down at him. *Silly me, I already have a protector.*

"Kaylee?" Nick's tone suggested he'd noticed her distraction. "Do you want to come over with us while Jessica locks up?"

Kaylee shook her head. "No, you go ahead. I'll lock up here and meet you out front."

"Are you sure?" Jessica asked.

"I'm fine, really. I'll check the doors as soon as you go out."

Nick insisted on making a quick run through the shop before he'd leave. Once that was done, Kaylee let him and Jessica outside to make the short walk to Death by Chocolate. She locked the door behind them, then put away the two unused mugs in the kitchen before walking out to the front counter, where there was a stash of treats for Bear. "You've earned this one," Kaylee said as she knelt to give it to him. "You're my hero."

Bear wolfed down the cookie eagerly, but showed even more excitement when Kaylee opened the front door for Nick. "We're ready to go," she said, leading Bear outside.

Nick moved aside so Kaylee could lock the door. "I must say, you're handling this well."

"I think I'm a little numb," Kaylee admitted as they walked to her SUV.

"That's to be expected. Do you want me to follow you home? I could check out the cottage and then stay while you lock up."

Kaylee patted his arm. "Thanks. You're a good friend and a good deputy. But Bear and I will be fine. I expect that man has delivered his message. I don't think he'll bother me again tonight."

"You're a brave lady, Kaylee Bleu," Nick said admiringly, and Kaylee forced a smile for him. If there was one thing she wasn't feeling, it was brave.

As she drove herself and Bear back to Wildflower Cottage, exhaustion seeped into her bones. She glanced at the clock on the dash, expecting to find it was late. To her surprise, the numbers showed barely eight. "This has been one long day," she told Bear.

As if in agreement, he gave a quick yip.

Kaylee watched the road ahead and noticed the side road that she knew would take her to Robin's Nest. On impulse, she turned off. "I bet you'd enjoy a visit with Gilbert and Sullivan." Kaylee hoped to ask Belinda about the mysterious stagehand. Rhett had clearly recognized her description and now that the man had threatened her, Kaylee felt it was more important than ever to find out who he was. If Belinda knew him, she was much more likely to tell Kaylee than her surly husband had been. "Of course, that's assuming Rhett doesn't slam the door in our faces when we get to the cottage."

Belinda's face lit up when she opened the door to Kaylee and Bear. "Sullivan is going to be so happy to see you! Come in. Can I make you a cup of tea? I just put on the electric kettle. I can't drink coffee after five or I don't sleep a wink, and decaf is gross. But tea is good whether it has caffeine or not."

"Tea sounds wonderful." Kaylee followed Belinda through the cottage to the small kitchen. Along the way, Kaylee admired a few interesting sculptures on shelves and side tables. She stopped short at one piece, a stylized metal horse rearing from the waves.

"I love that one," Belinda said, her eyes shining. "Though I haven't found exactly the right place for it yet." She laughed lightly. "I move pieces from room to room until I find the perfect home for them. It drives poor Rhett up the wall."

When they got to the kitchen, Kaylee could see Belinda's artistic touch there as well. The walls were painted a soft blue, and with the bright yellow accent pieces Belinda had added, the room had a cheerful homeyness. Kaylee sat at the small table, and Bear plopped down next to her.

At the sound of nails scuttling on the floor, Bear barked once before Sullivan skidded around the corner. The two dogs greeted one another with wagging tails and enthusiastic sniffs.

"I knew Sullivan would be thrilled," Belinda said as she set mugs on the counter. She dropped in tea bags.

"Is Rhett home?" Kaylee asked—not that she wanted to chat with the man, but she didn't want any sudden surprises. Her day had held enough of those.

"He stayed late at the theater with Gilbert," Belinda said as she poured hot water into the mugs. "He said he wanted to work on the play. There are things he didn't feel were right yet."

"It must be exciting, putting on a play you created yourselves," Kaylee said.

"Exciting and scary." Belinda carried the mugs to the table and slipped into the seat across from Kaylee. "Sometimes it's more one than the other."

"Today has been full of scary moments. I assume you heard about Rhett's near miss from the car?"

"I did. Not that Rhett told me. Quinn called and caught me

up. I called Rhett, but he insists he's fine." She leaned closer to Kaylee. "You saw him. Did he seem okay? He can be such a baby about doctors."

"He had a few scrapes, but I think he's fine. He'll be feeling a little stiff though."

Belinda's eyes filled with tears. "Rhett and I have been having some trouble since we moved here, but I was shocked that he didn't call me himself when he came so close to real injury. What's happening to us?"

Kaylee reached out to pat the other woman's hand. "Maybe he didn't want to worry you. He kept insisting it wasn't a big deal at the time."

"Maybe." Belinda wiped at her eyes with a napkin from the table, then took a sip of her tea. She was obviously putting a lot of effort into calming down, so Kaylee waited quietly, drinking from her own cup.

"Earlier, you said scary *moments*," Belinda said after a brief silence. "What else happened?"

"Well, during the auditions, I saw a strange man backstage. I thought he was a stagehand because he was dressed all in black, but I've been told you haven't hired any stage crew yet."

"I've hired them," Belinda said. "But they won't be coming out until a couple weeks before the performance." She sighed deeply. "It's a cost-saving thing. I expect the person you saw was probably there to audition. Maybe he thought all black was a good fashion choice?"

"Maybe," Kaylee said. "I wonder if you might recognize him." She described the man, taking special care to mention the scar. No sign of recognition flickered on Belinda's face, though she frowned slightly.

"I don't remember anyone with a scar auditioning," she said. "I would have noticed that since it would be something we'd have to cover with makeup. How very odd. Maybe it was a friend or spouse of someone who auditioned? There were so many people. I might not have seen all of them."

"Or maybe it was the man who attacked Delia," Kaylee suggested.

Belinda sat up sharply. "Do you think so?"

"I do. Tonight, he was lurking in the dark when I took Bear for a walk behind my shop. He threatened us and told me not to poke into things at the theater."

"That doesn't make sense," Belinda insisted. "Why would someone threaten you? You're not a member of the troupe, and you're barely even in the play."

"I don't know, but I described the man to your husband. Rhett said he didn't recognize him, but I'm not sure he was telling the truth."

Bear had been roughhousing with Sullivan but something in Kaylee's tone alerted him, and he left the other dog to sit by her. Sullivan followed him, and soon Kaylee had a dachshund leaning on each ankle.

Belinda's expression became distressed and she fidgeted with her mug. "I wish I could stoutly defend Rhett's honesty, but he's been behaving so oddly lately. He's become secretive. I've even wondered if there might be another woman, though I'm fairly sure that's not the case. Honestly, he's a handsome man and we're actors. He's had plenty of women show interest in him, but he's only ever had eyes for me."

"But he is acting oddly," Kaylee prompted.

"He's done things that are out of character, like all the worry about remodeling costs. You see, I'm from a well-to-do family and I get a rather large allowance from my parents. On top of that, there's a trust fund from my grandmother that kicked in after Rhett and I were married last year. Money is not an issue, not even a little bit. Even if the theater failed spectacularly, we'd still be fine, so I don't know why he's suddenly so concerned about it."

"Maybe he feels worrying about money is part of being a husband," Kaylee said. "Did the stress on your relationship begin after the wedding?"

Belinda set her empty mug down and pushed it away from her. "Not immediately after. At first, everything was wonderful. I didn't expect it to be so magical. Rhett and I had been together for years, so I thought being married would be almost anticlimactic, but it wasn't. It was amazing for months." Her cheeks pinked. "We've even talked about starting a family. That's part of what motivated the move here. I want my kids to have roots."

"You said it was amazing for months—did anything happen after that?"

Belinda shifted uncomfortably. "Rhett started acting strange. Fretting about money. Disappearing sometimes. The only thing we agreed about completely was moving here. He may question our expenses, but he loved the idea of moving to Turtle Cove, especially with the possibility of starting a family."

That surprised Kaylee. "Had he been here before?"

"No, but I had. My grandmother brought me here once when I was little. We went on a whale watch, and I was amazed by everything. I knew someday I wanted to live here, at least part of the year. But Rhett had never even heard of Turtle Cove."

"I would think it'd be a tough choice for an actor though," Kaylee asked. "It's not exactly a hub of theater activity."

Belinda laughed. "Not yet, but you wait. It will be. Our play is good, and with some positive reviews of our first few productions, we could be a summer destination." She smiled bigger.

"That would be great," Kaylee said, though she wasn't sure Turtle Cove was quite ready to become the Broadway of the Pacific Northwest.

Belinda's cheeks pinked again. "I love the idea of our theater being a legacy for our children. It's one of the reasons why I wanted everything about it to be perfect. It's been an uphill battle with Rhett nagging me about money."

"Are you sure the problem *is* strictly money?" Kaylee asked. "Maybe Rhett is worried about becoming a father and it's coming out as fretting about money."

Belinda began spinning her mug absently. "Maybe. I don't know." She sighed. "Rhett and I always had our separate interests. I thought that actually made us stronger." She waved toward a shelf on the wall that held delicate glass sculptures. "For instance, my passion for art. Rhett isn't into that, so I don't ask him to go to art galleries or antiques shops with me. Rhett, on the other hand, prefers spending the occasional weekend with old college buddies, and that was fine, mostly. I think they go fishing or something manly like that."

"Have you met these college friends?"

"A couple of them, but not all of them. Most of the socializing they do involves going off to the woods to sleep on the ground. I'm not into that."

Kaylee had to admit, she preferred her bed at night too. "Has he gone on any of these outings since you moved here?"

Belinda shook her head. "Not one. A few months after the wedding, he started hanging out with these guys a lot more often. He virtually used up all the time we weren't tied to a production schedule with them. I was feeling a little neglected, actually." She huffed and stood up to gather mugs. "Then we started talking about a family and moved here. I hate to admit it, but one of the things I love about Orcas Island is having more distance between Rhett and his buddies. Now his time with them will take some planning, and that will leave more time for Rhett and me together. Working on the theater has kept us busy."

"But not altogether happy." Kaylee watched Belinda carry the mugs to the sink. When the actress faced her again, Kaylee asked, "Has Rhett said much about the mysterious lilies?"

Belinda leaned forward on the kitchen's butcher block island. "He's more creeped out by them than I am. Secret admirers aren't exactly unheard of when you're an actress, even one as little known as I am. But the flowers started bothering Rhett after Delia's accident. Though lately, everything seems to be an excuse to fight."

Kaylee saw a faraway stare glaze Belinda's eyes again, and she bent to stroke Bear's head, giving the other woman time to compose herself.

"Would you like some lemon cake?" Belinda asked, snapping back into the moment. "I made it myself. I bake when I'm stressed."

"It's good to have an outlet. I arrange flowers." Kaylee stood. "I'm going to have to pass on the cake though. I should get home. I think Bear and I are about worn out."

"Thanks for coming by. I haven't been very good company, but I appreciate your kindness." Then Belinda's false cheer slipped a bit. "It was nice to talk. I can't share my problems with the others in the troupe since Rhett and I are their leaders. It feels disloyal to unload, but sometimes I need someone to talk to."

"You can always call me," Kaylee said. "Or come by the shop. I'm happy to listen."

"It helps me feel better," Belinda said sadly, "but I don't know of anything that will help the situation. I thought the theater was going to bring Rhett and me together again, but I'm starting to worry that it's all too late."

Kaylee wished she had something encouraging to say to that, but she was entirely afraid that Belinda was right. Something was brewing in the secrets Rhett was keeping, and Kaylee didn't think that whatever he was hiding would be good for anyone.

14

The rest of the ride to Wildflower Cottage was quiet. Bear feel asleep immediately, so Kaylee didn't process the thoughts swirling through her head out loud. One thing she knew was that she'd be glad to get home. But when she pulled into her driveway, she realized how very dark the island could be this far from town, and she was frightened by the secretive shadows around her property. This late in the year, there were no insect sounds, just the crash of waves in the distance.

She collected Bear and let herself into the cottage long enough to switch on all the lights, then addressed Bear's purposeful stares at the door. "You already had a walk at the bakery, remember?"

Bear wagged his tail with enthusiasm.

"Fine, a short walk."

She grabbed her heavy coat from the peg rack near the door and followed her dog out into the darkness. She tried to focus on how peaceful the quiet usually felt to her, but her nerves were having none of it. "I'm not being paranoid!" Her voice sounded too loud in the night, and Bear jerked his head up sharply in concern.

If that guy knows I visited Belinda, he'd have to know I'm not leaving things alone with the theater. Kaylee peered around, wishing she could see. It felt as if the cottage's lighting barely nudged the darkness. All it did was spotlight her and Bear if the scarred stranger was watching her.

Despite her mounting nerves, Kaylee let Bear sniff around the flower beds near the house for a few more minutes before coaxing him inside sooner than usual. Thankfully, the dog had also had a full day and didn't resist.

Once inside, she checked the locks on all the doors and windows. She was annoyed with herself for letting the stranger win. This must be exactly the fear he had been hoping to induce, but she couldn't seem to do much about it.

The landline rang, shattering the oppressive silence in the cottage and making her jump. "I'm handling this so well," she grumbled as she headed for the phone.

She picked up the receiver, and the voice she heard was the soothing balm she needed. "Sorry for calling late," her grandmother said. "I hope I didn't wake you."

Until she heard Bea's voice, Kaylee hadn't realized how much she had been missing her. Bea Lyons lived in Arizona now, and Kaylee knew how much her grandmother loved it, but that didn't mean she didn't miss her even more during tough times.

"No, I just got in," Kaylee said, forcing herself not to cry. "And there is nothing I would rather do than talk to you right now."

"Oh dear, that sounds dire."

"I'm probably overreacting a little." Kaylee sniffled, then went on to tell Bea about the theater and everything that had happened. She couldn't stop a few tears from slipping down her cheeks, but she tried to keep the lump in her throat from showing in her voice.

"You must be scared half to death," Bea said finally. "I know I would be. Maybe you and Bear should heed that man's warning and stay away from the theater. That couple has both dogs again, and I don't think you owe them anything."

"I might," Kaylee said quietly, then she gave a weak laugh. "Nick told me I was brave. I don't feel brave. I'd happily forget all about this, but Polly and Zoe are in the play. Plus, I've grown fond of Belinda, and if something happened to any of them, I'd feel terrible about abandoning them. I don't know what I think I can do to protect them, but I'll feel better being there."

Bea sighed into the phone. "I'd probably feel the same way. And I happen to agree with Nick—you *are* brave. Brave isn't about how you feel, sweetheart. It's about what you do. And you always do the right thing by your friends."

The warmth of her grandmother's approval made Kaylee feel better than she had for hours. "Thanks, Grandma. Now, I've talked about myself ever since I answered the phone. I haven't even given you a chance to tell me why you called."

"I mostly called because I was feeling a little achy and knew I wouldn't get to sleep quickly. But I also want to make sure you're doing something nice for Thanksgiving. Since we're not getting together this year, I want to make sure you're taken care of."

"I will be," Kaylee promised. "DeeDee has invited me to have Thanksgiving with them. The girls make every get-together an event, so I'm sure it'll be fun. Speaking which, I still need to ask DeeDee what I can bring." Kaylee sighed. "The holidays really snuck up on me this year."

Bea laughed. "They sneak up on me every year, though I'm nearly done with the cardigan I'm knitting Isabella for Christmas."

Kaylee groaned. Isabella was one of Kaylee's nieces, another person she hadn't gotten a gift for yet. "I've done almost no shopping," she said. "But Mary spent all evening tracking down some fun fishing gifts for Herb." And with that, they spent the rest of the call talking about the coming holidays and the people they loved. It was exactly what Kaylee's spirit needed.

When they finally hung up, Kaylee glanced at the clock on the wall and yelped. It was late and she needed a good night's sleep. There was no telling what the next day might hold. She checked the locks one more time, then scooped up Bear and headed for bed.

She was all the way into her room when she remembered that she needed to charge her phone. *I'm getting as bad as Reese.*

That reminded her that she hadn't seen a text from Reese yet, though she was sure he'd made it home safely just as she had. She walked out and fished the phone from her purse. The charge was so low that the phone wouldn't even turn on. She plugged it into the charger and headed for bed, hoping that a good night's sleep would recharge her internal battery as well.

Kaylee woke on Saturday morning to find Bear cuddled up against the small of her back and gentle sunlight filtering in through the windows. She yelped as she hopped out of bed. "Bear! We overslept."

She rushed through her morning routine, then snagged her phone from the charger before hustling Bear out to the car. Since the air still held plenty of the night chill, she let the motor warm up a little before leaving. She checked her phone while she waited and discovered two text messages.

The first was from Reese, letting her know that he had gotten home safe and sound. She felt a small rush of relief as she moved to the next text.

It had come in after her visit with Belinda, probably when the charge on her phone was too low for an alert. The message was short, but reading it made her stomach clench around the granola she'd wolfed down. From a blocked number, someone had sent four words:

You're not following orders.

Kaylee called Nick immediately and asked him to meet her at the shop. Once there, he read the message, his expression dark. "We might not be able to do much to track down the origin of the call. I'll try if you don't mind signing a release of your phone records."

"Anything to help," she said.

He patted her arm a little awkwardly. "You know, most people who act menacingly don't actually do anything about it."

"And I would take that to heart, except that someone pushed Delia down and nearly ran over Rhett." Kaylee sighed. "And then there's the dognapping of Sullivan."

"Any or all of those things could be unrelated," Nick said. "But I promise you we're still taking this seriously. I'm not the only deputy looking for this guy. We'll find him and we'll have a nice chat about what's going on. In the meanwhile, all you need to do is take normal precautions and try not to worry too much."

Kaylee offered a crooked smile. "I'll do my best."

Thankfully, the rest of the day at the shop was busy. The weather warmed hour by hour, luring many people out to enjoy the sunshine with some leisurely Main Street shopping. Kaylee sold not only all the small arrangements in the cooler, but also several that she made during the day. As customers kept her hopping, she had little time left for worry.

The weekend passed quietly with no more hints of danger, and Kaylee started to hope the warnings were going to be the end of things. After church on Sunday, she popped into The Flower Patch to refill the cooler with small arrangements, though she didn't open to customers. The quiet in the shop felt cozy instead of lonely, and Kaylee found that the meditative act of flower arranging worked its usual magic, leaving her positively optimistic by the time she went home with Bear.

Monday dawned bright and beautiful. It was even warmer than the weekend, with a stiff breeze but none of the bone-chilling cold that Kaylee knew would sweep in again soon. As they drove into town, she promised Bear a long walk at some point during the day. At the word *walk*, Bear wagged his tail with excitement.

"Maybe we'll even get in some Christmas shopping," Kaylee said.

Apparently Kaylee wasn't the only one inspired by the warm weather. The Flower Patch had foot traffic all morning, and most people left with either one of the small arrangements or some of DeeDee's homemade lavender goat milk soap.

"It's good to see you so relaxed," Mary said when they had a midmorning lull. "You were still a bit distracted when I saw you at church, though I can't blame you with those threats you received. I'd have felt better if you'd accepted my offer to come over after the service."

"You helped tremendously just by caring," Kaylee said warmly. "I'd be lost without you. I do feel better today. Church did me good. Somehow the message always seems to be exactly the one I need to hear."

"I've felt that way before," Mary agreed.

"It reminded me that I'm never alone, and I needed to remember that. When I came in to do some arrangements on Sunday afternoon, I know that sermon helped me feel safe here again."

The door to the shop swung open and Kaylee was surprised to see a small, reddish-brown head poke around the doorjamb. Then Sullivan pranced into the shop, followed by Belinda.

Bear gave a yip of pure joy and rushed to greet his friend.

"You've made Bear very happy," Kaylee told Belinda. She was surprised when the actress responded to that with a very weak smile. "What's wrong?"

Belinda's smile stretched wider but seemed even more brittle. "Nothing's wrong. Everything is great. Sullivan and Gilbert are acting completely normal. And that means we really don't need understudies at all. Plus, Bear isn't going to get over his tail-wagging every time he sees someone he knows. That could be a problem on stage. Though his friendliness is a lovely trait." She reached down to pat Bear while Kaylee processed what she'd just said.

"Are you firing Bear?"

Mary folded her arms over her chest and declared, "That is appalling."

Belinda laughed, a sound as false as her smile. "Of course we're not *firing* Bear. You always knew Sullivan would take the role again once we found him."

"Was eliminating a dog understudy your idea or your husband's?" Kaylee asked quietly.

"We agreed together," Belinda said, though her voice still sounded strained and she didn't quite meet Kaylee's eyes. Kaylee wished desperately that Belinda would tell her the truth. "And you must realize, we *love* Bear. We're so grateful to him for finding Sullivan."

Kaylee was pleased that at least the last bit of Belinda's speech sounded honest. But everything inside her told her there was no way Belinda actually wanted to get rid of them. Had something new happened? Had the mysterious stranger threatened her as well?

She laid a hand on the actress's arm. "Belinda, is something wrong?"

"No, nothing," Belinda said. "Sullivan and I need to dash. Tons of things to get done. Thanks again, and who knows? Maybe there will be a role for Bear in a different show."

The actress scooped up Sullivan and practically ran from the shop.

Mary frowned darkly at the door as it closed. "You'd think a professional actress would be a better liar."

"That performance was definitely flawed," Kaylee agreed. "I think Rhett is behind it. He doesn't want me at the theater." She drummed her fingers on the counter as she thought about it. Then she turned to Mary. "I wonder if he could be behind the threats to me. He might have put that man with the scar up to it."

"They could be working on something together," Mary suggested. "Something nefarious. Not that you'll be able to do much about it. It sounds as if you've been given the boot." She walked around to pat Bear. "Poor baby. You would have stolen the show, and they know it."

Bear gave her a big doggy grin.

The door opened again, and Mary straightened to greet Reese. "Hi there. I was about to put on a fresh pot of coffee. Do you want a cup?" she asked him.

"Now that's a full-service florist," Reese said with a smile. "Sure, I'd love some coffee. Thanks."

"You too?" Mary asked Kaylee.

"I'd better not," Kaylee said. "I've had a couple cups today, and I'm going to end up vibrating. Plus, the caffeine isn't exactly helping my nerves."

Once Mary walked to the kitchen, Reese crouched to pet Bear. "How you doing, big guy?"

Bear barked, wriggling all over from joy.

"He's doing great," Kaylee said. "He's always happy to see people who want to pet him. What are you up to today?"

With a final pat on Bear's head, Reese stood. "I've been out checking my patch on the theater security system. Apparently it worked, because no one has reported any flowers on the stage since I fixed it. The secret admirer must have been using the stage door."

"I'm glad something's going right for the theater," Kaylee said. "They've had more than their share of problems."

Reese's expression grew concerned. "I'm sensing subtext. Did something happen?"

"A few things, actually," Kaylee admitted. She caught him

up on the threats and Belinda's strange visit.

"Why didn't you tell me before?" he asked. "Is Nick aware of all this? I should come out and check out the cottage to make sure all the locks are strong. I could add some new dead bolts if you want."

"Nick knows about everything except Belinda's visit this morning, and I'm not calling him about that. And I have plenty of locks." Kaylee took a deep breath, trying not to let Reese's alarm stir her worries up. "I've been fine, really. And now apparently Bear and I won't be going to any more rehearsals, so at least you won't have to watch out for us there."

"Belinda's visit worries me," Reese said. "It doesn't sound like her. I thought Bear was her hero."

"So did I. But something is going on at the theater, and clearly I'm not wanted. On the upside, that should mean no one has any reason to threaten me anymore."

"It doesn't make me feel better that someone did that in the first place." Reese rubbed his chin. "But I'm glad you two won't be spending time at the theater now. Maybe it's all over."

Kaylee forced a smile though she couldn't quite share his optimism. Whatever was going on, she was pretty sure it wasn't over. Not by a long shot.

15

Though Bear's role in the play had been cut, Kaylee couldn't help but fret about DeeDee and her girls. The worry distracted her while she worked on more small arrangements for the browsing cooler, and she realized the only answer was to simply talk to DeeDee. So when it was time to take Bear for a walk, she snapped the leash on him and headed for the mystery bookstore DeeDee owned down the street.

When she walked into Between the Lines, she was surprised to find DeeDee's husband, Andy, leaning on the front counter, talking to his wife. They both grinned as Kaylee and Bear came in. Andy ambled over and rubbed Bear's ears, much to the dog's delight.

"I hear you're coming to Thanksgiving," Andy said to Kaylee. "The girls are over the moon about it. Polly said she had thought Thanksgiving was going to be boring, but it'll be better with Bear around."

"I can't imagine life ever being boring around your house," Kaylee said. "Which reminds me, what can I bring?"

"What would you like to bring?" DeeDee asked as Andy returned to the counter. He whispered something in her ear, and her eyes lit up. "Oh, do you have Bea's recipe for corn bread stuffing with sausage in it? She said it was a family secret, but you *are* family."

"I'll call and ask her for it," Kaylee said. "Pencil me in for Grandma's stuffing."

"Excellent," Andy said, slapping a hand on the counter. "Now I'm with Polly and Zoe. This is going to be the best Thanksgiving ever!"

His little girl imitation made Kaylee laugh. "I wish everything I came to tell you was met with as much enthusiasm."

DeeDee's smile evaporated. "What? Did something happen?"

Kaylee nodded solemnly. "A couple things actually, and I thought you should be aware of them since your girls are in the play."

DeeDee and Andy exchanged a serious expression. "I don't like the sound of that," Andy said.

Kaylee felt terrible about ruining their good mood, but she told them about the dark events at the theater anyway. They had a right to know, especially since their daughters were involved in the play. DeeDee's body language tightened as she listened.

"That's horrible," DeeDee said at last, her voice nearly a whisper. She reached out and took Andy's hand. "I'm not sure about the girls being around the theater. There's a rehearsal Wednesday night, and I'm feeling uncomfortable with them going now."

"I admit what happened to Kaylee is concerning," Andy said. "But there's not much reason to suspect that it puts the girls in any danger. What did Nick say?"

"He's not enthusiastic about the play," Kaylee said. "And the threats aren't the only thing I need to tell you about. Bear and I were kicked out of the play today. Belinda came by and said they don't need a dachshund understudy anymore. She was absolutely miserable while she told me. I think the idea came from Rhett. He's not a fan of me."

"That's it," DeeDee announced, waving her hands. "The girls are out of that play." Andy reached out to put a hand on her arm, but she backed away. "Don't try to change my mind."

"You've heard Polly and Zoe," he said gently. "How do you think they're going to take this? What if I go with all of you to every rehearsal? One of us could stay in the audience and one in the wings."

"There are two wings," DeeDee said. "And when the girls

exit the stage, they split and each go to a separate wing."

"Fine," he said. "We'll each stand in one of the wings."

"Then who will watch from the audience?" DeeDee asked. "The girls will be just as hurt not to have anyone out in the audience." She pointed at Kaylee. "I will go along with it on a trial basis for Wednesday night, but only if you come too. You could help keep an eye on the girls."

"I'm not sure they'll even let me in," Kaylee said.

"If they won't, then they won't get my girls either, and they can deal with the mighty upheaval that will cause," DeeDee said, her voice firm. "Bring Bear. He can sniff out trouble better than anyone I know. If he acts relaxed, I'll feel a good bit better."

"I'll try," Kaylee agreed. "But as I said, I'm not sure if they'll let me in." Then she smiled. "Reese has been doing handyman work for the theater. We could have him come too. With the four of us, the girls will be as safe as if they were in their own beds." Bear barked at Kaylee, and she glanced down at him. "What?"

Andy laughed and knelt again. "He thinks you miscounted. With Reese, it'll be *five* of us. Right, Wonder Dog?"

Bear barked again. Kaylee suspected he'd been feeling left out with so much conversation and so little petting, but she enjoyed the light moment. She hoped they'd have more of them in the days ahead.

On Wednesday after work, Kaylee pulled into the parking lot at the theater and cut the engine. She stared at the building for a moment, working up her courage. She'd never enjoyed personal drama or conflict, and now she was getting ready to walk into a situation that was definitely going to provoke at least one person and maybe more.

"I need to think about Zoe and Polly," she announced, then hopped out of the SUV quickly before she could change her mind and drive home. Bear clearly had none of her misgivings and wriggled with excitement as she snapped on his leash and headed for the door.

She found Quinn in the lobby. The young actress spotted Kaylee and came to greet them with a smile. "There's the handsomest guy in town," Quinn declared as she bent to pet the little dog.

Kaylee was glad to see that Rhett's antipathy toward Kaylee hadn't spread to the whole troupe. Then she thought of something she hadn't considered. "Quinn, could I ask you a personal question? It's going to sound weird, but I promise it's important."

The young actress peered at her curiously. "Sure. I'm an open book. What do you want to know?"

"Could you describe your ex-boyfriend? Was he older than you?"

Clearly the question surprised Quinn and her expression grew wary. "A couple years. Not much. He's not much taller than me, wiry, and he has black hair."

Not the mystery man. "Does he have a scar?" Kaylee asked, just to be sure. She brushed her fingers over her cheek. "Right here?"

Quinn shook her head. "No, Jason would die if he had a scar marring his face. He is more than a little vain." She sighed deeply. "Sometimes I wonder what I ever saw in him."

"So he doesn't contact you at all?"

Quinn's gaze dropped to Bear. "Of course not. Aunt Belinda would freak, and I don't want to lose my job here."

"I'm sure she wouldn't fire you over something like that," Kaylee said, wondering at Quinn's sudden unwillingness to meet her gaze.

"What are *you* doing here?" Rhett demanded. The door to

the auditorium swung shut behind him.

From the corner of her eye, Kaylee saw DeeDee, Andy, and the girls walk into the lobby from the parking lot. She gestured toward them. "I came to support DeeDee and her girls."

"We aren't inviting the public in for these rehearsals," Rhett snapped.

"Kaylee isn't the public," DeeDee said. "She's family. Our family. And we're more than a little nervous about the strange goings-on here, so I want as much family around my girls as possible."

"There are no strange goings-on here," Rhett practically shouted. "She's blown everything out of proportion, and she's a distraction to the work we do here." He flapped a hand at DeeDee and Andy. "Your children have the two of you. That's plenty."

"Why is he being so *mean*?" Polly wailed before bursting into tears, and Bear began barking furiously at Rhett. More people were coming into the theater for the rehearsal, but stopped and stared when they heard the commotion. Clearly the show Rhett was putting on was more interesting than anything else.

DeeDee put her arm around her daughter. "I'll thank you not to yell around my children. They're not used to adults making fools of themselves."

The doors leading from the lobby to the auditorium opened again, and Belinda walked out, then hurried over to where the crowd had formed. Quinn intercepted her and whispered to her aunt.

"I don't want to cause trouble," Kaylee said. "But I intend to stay and help watch over Zoe and Polly as long as they are here."

"Certainly," Belinda said firmly as she closed the distance to stand by her husband. "I am sorry for ever giving in to suggestions that you don't belong in the theater." She scowled at her husband. "You and Bear saved Sullivan, and there is no way either of you will ever be barred from *my* theater." Her tone was so firm that Kaylee almost expected her to punctuate her words with a stomp of her foot. Quinn stood off to one side of the group, grinning proudly at her aunt.

"Thank you," Kaylee said quietly.

Rhett looked from Belinda to Kaylee and back again. Finally he waved a hand in the air. "Fine. Don't blame me if we end up with more drama!" Then he stormed away.

"The only one causing drama here was him," DeeDee muttered before turning her attention to soothing Polly.

Belinda took Kaylee's hand. "Forgive me for being a rotten friend?"

"There's nothing to forgive," Kaylee said gently. "You were in a tough spot."

"All the more reason for me to get tougher." Then Belinda clapped her hands loudly. "Let's get this rehearsal on the road." She whirled and herded her cast into the theater.

As Kaylee led Bear in, she felt a tug at her arm. She glanced down to see Polly slip her small hand into Kaylee's. "I'm glad that mean man didn't make you leave," the little girl whispered loudly.

"Me too," Kaylee whispered back, getting a bright smile from the little girl.

Everyone settled into seats near the stage to wait for each scene to be called. Belinda walked out onto the stage to announce the beginning of the rehearsal. "I have some wonderful news tonight," she said. "Delia is here and will be taking up her role in *Midsummer Madness*."

Belinda applauded and the others joined in as Delia walked out and took a quick bow. The large bandage was gone from Delia's head, but when she bowed, Kaylee spotted a smaller one behind the actress's right ear.

Reese slipped into the seat beside Kaylee as Belinda was going over the scene list planned for the rehearsal. "Quinn said I missed some fireworks out front."

"A little bit," Kaylee replied. "I don't think I'm at the top of Rhett's list of favorite people."

"Then he's not on my list at all. How can I like someone who has such poor taste in people?"

Finally, Kaylee was able to smile.

When the scene the Wilcox girls were in was called, Kaylee and the others had a quick whispered discussion about which of them should go where. "I should probably stay out of the backstage unless you need me there," Kaylee said quietly. "I don't want to give Rhett more reason to get worked up."

"That's not a problem," Reese said. "I think Andy and I should take the wings. No one will get by us."

DeeDee's gaze shifted between them. "I think you're right. I'll stay here with Kaylee and applaud like crazy."

"Good plan," Andy agreed. He stood and followed Zoe out of the row. Polly was already in the aisle, bouncing up and down impatiently.

"I hope I don't regret this," DeeDee said as she watched the girls walk to the stage with Reese and Andy on either side.

"I don't think the guys will let anything happen to them," Kaylee reassured her friend.

"You're right, of course," DeeDee agreed, though her voice was laced with tension.

The girls were great, as Kaylee had expected. Since neither Sullivan nor Gilbert ran to Polly, she didn't have to resist the urge to pet them and stayed on task with her jacks, while her sister did a very convincing job of pretend-arguing with her friend Meghan. As the rehearsal continued smoothly, Kaylee finally began to relax. *Maybe the weirdness is really over.*

The girls' scene wrapped without incident, but Belinda asked the cast to stay. "We may have time to run through that scene again at the end."

Kaylee scooted down one seat so Zoe and Polly could sit on each side of their mom. Zoe announced that it was her turn to sit by Bear, so Andy sat on the other side of Polly.

"Is Reese coming?" DeeDee asked.

"He told me he wanted to watch the rest of the rehearsal from the wings for safety's sake," Andy replied.

"What a guy," DeeDee said with a small grin and a quick glance at Kaylee, who rolled her eyes.

The rehearsal stretched late, and Kaylee noticed Polly nodding sleepily. Eventually, she fell asleep on her mother's shoulder.

Polly wasn't the only one feeling the long rehearsal. Bear began to grow fidgety and Kaylee leaned toward Zoe. "I'm going to take Bear for a walk," Kaylee whispered. "Please tell your mom."

Kaylee took Bear up the aisle and into the backstage area. She intended to slip out the back door and let Bear walk a little while on the patch of brown grass. She didn't know of any other grass in that part of the waterfront and didn't want Bear walking too much on the cold sidewalks at night. Though it was far from the temperatures they'd see in winter, she worried that it might be cold enough to freeze his paw pads.

She didn't see Reese backstage and assumed he was in the wings on the other side of the stage. She continued down the darkened hallway and pushed open the backstage door, only to groan at the sight of drizzling rain. She was wearing a decently warm jacket and even had a hood, but she didn't have an umbrella.

Bear sniffed the rainy air hopefully, making her decision for her. She pulled his small rain poncho from her purse and slipped it on him, snapping the poncho hood under his chin next to his blue-and-white chevron bow tie. Figuring they were as protected as she could manage, she let Bear lead her outside.

The rain was chilly but barely more than a mist, and the theater building blocked the wind, so it wasn't nearly as bad as Kaylee had expected. She pulled the hood up on her jacket to keep icy trickles from running down her back. "If you could hurry," she told Bear, "that would be great."

If Bear understood the request, he showed no sign of complying. Instead, he snuffled through the grass thoroughly. At least he didn't seem interested in leaving the immediate area.

Suddenly, he abandoned his olfactory exploration and stood at attention, his nose pointed toward the darkness. He began growling deep in his chest.

Kaylee remembered how he'd barked at the intruder behind the shop. "Bear," she said, tugging the leash. "Let's get inside."

Instead of complying, Bear launched into a volley of angry barks and lunged forward. Though she'd thought she had a good grip on the leash, the combination of cold fingers and rain-slick leather was enough to let the little dog pull the leash out of Kaylee's hand. He took off, still barking.

"Bear!"

She started after him, but someone shoved her hard from behind, knocking her to the ground. Before she could scramble to her feet, something heavy slammed into her back, bringing a burst of pain with it and flattening her.

A hoarse voice snarled into her ear.

"You were warned."

16

The heavy weight pressed sharply into Kaylee's back and she struggled against it, expecting to be struck again at any moment. Whatever pinned her stank of earthy rot. No further blows came, only the weight pushing her into the soggy, dirty ground. She realized she couldn't get enough leverage to lift up the hefty item, so she dragged herself forward instead. The thing pressing on her scraped down her backbone as she inched along.

The rain increased from mist to sharp pellets, and the ground around her quickly transformed into a swamp. Her progression could be measured in inches, as the bone-chilling cold slowed her nearly as much as the weight. She finally crawled far enough forward that the weight pushed on her legs instead of her back. It still hurt, but she could move more quickly and was soon out, gasping as she rolled over and peered into the darkness to determine what had pinned her. It was the old picnic table, now canted on its side.

Kaylee struggled to her feet. She was fairly certain she wasn't seriously injured, but she was in pain nonetheless. She could feel raw scrapes down her back, and her hip ached, though she wasn't sure what had caused that. She also suspected one knee must have hit a rock when she fell because it felt swollen and hot through her jeans. On top of everything, she was wet and very cold. She knew the best thing would be to go inside where she could get help, but Bear was alone in the dark. There was no way she was leaving him.

"Bear!" she hollered as she limped in the same direction she'd gone with Bear on the night they'd found Sullivan. *Please let this night have a happy ending too.*

The rain softened the mud that clung to her, and she brushed it away from her arms and face as she limped along. She had to catch up to Bear soon because she could sense the cold slowing her down, making her mind feel as thick as the mud in her hair. She needed help.

Kaylee stopped suddenly and pulled her phone out of her pocket, holding her breath and hoping the attack hadn't broken it. She nearly sobbed with relief when the screen lit up, and she saw she had phone service. If she'd gone much farther, she might not have.

She quickly texted Reese, since calling him would definitely lead to a prolonged conversation where he'd be sure to insist on her coming back. *Someone attacked me behind theater. I'm okay. Bear missing. I'm searching.*

Before she could even shove the phone in her jeans pocket, it buzzed with Reese's response. *Where?*

Kaylee typed back a short note of her own: *Shed.* She wasn't there yet, but she knew where she was heading. She hoped that Bear would be following the scents he'd tracked before, especially since the shed probably still smelled of Sullivan. As she limped through the darkness, she tried to picture him sitting next to the tiny shack in his little poncho, his head tilted as he watched her walk up. He'd give her that look, the one that asked what had taken her so long.

Kaylee nearly screamed when a large shadow broke free from a building up ahead. She wiped water from her face with her forearm, feeling the gritty dirt it left behind. "Reese?" she asked.

"No, miss," a deep voice said. "The name's John Horne. Are you all right? This isn't a night for a walk."

Kaylee didn't know anyone by that name, but the voice sounded kind. Still, that hardly meant she was safe, so she didn't move any closer. "I'm searching for my dog."

"A dog?" the man repeated. "I expect your dog is better suited for this weather than you are. You ought to get inside." She heard footsteps and the man's hulking shadow grew bigger, and she backed away.

"I have to find my dog," she insisted. She knew she was in no shape to run, but the man was standing between her and Bear. And suddenly she felt very angry. "Please move. I need to go that way." She pointed, though she doubted the man could see any better in the darkness than she could.

"I don't want to leave a lady alone out here in the dark," the man said. "And I'm not sure you're thinking clearly."

"If you don't let me pass, I'm going to scream."

She saw the shadow lurch away from her. "No need for that, miss. I only want to help."

"That's good of you, sir," a familiar voice said from behind Kaylee. One she knew well. "But I've got this."

"Reese," Kaylee said, relief flooding her so hard that her knees nearly buckled.

"Is that right, miss?" the stranger asked, his voice still kind. "Do you know this man?"

"Yes, this is Reese Holt, a friend," Kaylee said.

"I'm John Horne," the stranger said. "You best get your lady friend inside, son. She sounds done in."

"I will. Thanks, John," Reese said.

Kaylee felt a coat being wrapped around her and a hood pulled up to cover her hair. She hadn't even noticed her own hood had fallen away.

The stranger merged into the shadows as Reese tried to coax Kaylee along. "We need to get you inside," he said. "You're shivering."

"Not until I find Bear," she insisted, though she could hear how her shivering made the words shake. "I think he might be at the shed where we found Sullivan."

"Kaylee, I want a doctor to look at you," Reese insisted.

"Not until I find Bear!" She yanked free of him so hard she nearly fell again. She had to locate her little dog.

"Okay, fine," Reese said. He put an arm around her, offering warmth and support. "But only as far as the shed. Then we're taking shelter whether you want to or not."

Kaylee decided to fight that fight when she came to it. As she limped along beside Reese, she was tempted to tell him to run ahead. He could move faster than she could, but she doubted he would leave her.

"Who attacked you? Did you see him?" he asked as they continued at a slow pace that made Kaylee want to scream with frustration. Dark, heavy fear was beginning to pool in her belly.

"No, I was hit from behind," she said. "But Bear went after someone who was ahead of me. That means there must have been two people. I didn't see either of them, but the person behind me must have come from inside the theater."

"Maybe," Reese said. "Or someone could have circled around you in the dark."

"I can't imagine why anyone would."

"Me neither, but I don't see why anyone would attack you in the first place. How badly are you hurt? And don't say, 'it's nothing,' because I can feel how much you're limping."

"The person pushed the old picnic table over on me after knocking me down," Kaylee said. "I've got some bruises, but I don't think it's anything serious. You were inside watching over Polly and Zoe. Did you see anyone sneak away?"

Reese sighed beside her. "No, but my attention was on the stage. I checked the security system right after we got there. The alarm was off so people could go out the stage door, but the system was still working."

"It wouldn't have kept anyone inside from getting outside to attack me," Kaylee said.

"No, but this system has some extra features," Reese said. "It actually records the time for every opening of every outside door. It does that whether the system is armed or not. The only reason it didn't work before was because of the rewiring. Tonight, it was functional."

Kaylee tried to work out what Reese was telling her, but her worry about Bear, her exhaustion, and the cold were making her thoughts feel sluggish. "I don't see how that helps," she said finally.

"We can determine for sure if whoever attacked you came from inside the theater," Reese said. "Because if they did, they had to open that door to come out. The records will show that."

"But it won't show who," Kaylee said.

"No, but it will show that it happened. And you should know that I called Nick as I was leaving the theater. I told him to meet us at the shed."

Kaylee was too tired to decide if she was relieved or annoyed by that, so she kept silent and put all her energy into setting one foot in front of the other. Bear had to be waiting at the shed. He had to be.

She couldn't even consider the possibility that he wasn't.

As tired as she was, an errant thought intruded as the sound of the water slapping against the pier came through the darkness. They were almost at the shed, and Kaylee was distracted by one truly strange thing. Why did her little dog run away when she was being attacked? That wasn't like Bear at all.

Kaylee felt her knees give way suddenly, but Reese held her up. "Kaylee," he said. "Are you all right? The shed is right there."

She poured the full force of her will into standing and her knees obliged. She stumbled toward the small building. "Bear!" Her voice was thin, wheezy, but she knew it would be enough if Bear was there. No bark answered her. Her second shout was little more than a sob. "Bear!"

The shed door hung ajar, but no little dog rushed toward her. "Let's get you inside out of the rain," Reese said. "We'll wait for Nick here."

Kaylee didn't have the energy to argue, her disappointment at not finding Bear draining what little strength she had left. Reese pulled her into the shed, and she felt the small relief of no more rain drumming against her. Reese began vigorously rubbing her hands between his own, offering her what little warmth he could.

"I was sure he'd be here," she whispered.

"That shows Bear had sense enough to find shelter earlier," Reese said. "He might even be at the theater, waiting for you."

Kaylee felt a surge of hope. "Do you think so?"

"Maybe." Reese raised her hands to his face and she could feel his breath against her skin. "Stay with me, Kaylee."

"I'm not going anywhere," she answered, though she felt suddenly so very tired. Only her worry about Bear kept her on her feet.

A moment later, a bright light flooded the shed, making Kaylee blink.

"Kaylee!" Nick's voice was sharp with concern. "Reese, why haven't you gotten her to a doctor yet?"

"Have you tried making Kaylee do something she doesn't want to do?" Reese asked him mildly. "She was sure Bear would be here at the shed."

"It wasn't a bad guess," Nick said.

Kaylee saw the light move over the walls of the shed and she followed it with her eyes, not having the energy for much else. The light fell on a long, thin knife stuck into the wood at eye level. That knife hadn't been there when they found Sullivan, Kaylee knew that. Neither had the note that it pinned to the wall.

Kaylee lurched away from Reese so she could peer closely at the paper. She nearly fell as she stumbled the few feet toward the wall, and had to reach out to brace herself. The note was written in plain block letters. The message was short.

We have the dog. $300,000 to get it back. Details to follow.

"Someone dognapped Bear," Reese said.
"Bear," Kaylee whispered, just before everything went black.

17

Kaylee came to before the ambulance arrived, and she immediately struggled against the thin blanket someone had wrapped around her. She was sitting in the shed, her back against one wall, making her sharply aware of the scrapes on her skin. The shed was better lit now, and Kaylee assumed that the electric lantern and the blanket around her were emergency supplies Nick kept in his car.

Then it hit her. Bear was missing. Dognapped. "Bear!" she yelled, struggling against the blanket that now felt more like a restraint than a comfort.

Reese was at her side in an instant. "It's going to be okay. We'll find him."

Nick stood in the doorway of the shed. "An ambulance is on the way."

"No!" Kaylee wrestled with the blanket. "I have to go find Bear."

Nick walked over and knelt in front of her. "That's my job now. Your job is to make sure you're okay. That's what the ambulance is for. You've been attacked, and then you tried to freeze to death while walking on a bad knee and probably making it worse."

Kaylee rolled her eyes. "I'm fine. Bruised, but fine. I'll see my own doctor tomorrow if that will make you happy, but I'm not going to the hospital now."

She fought to stand, and Reese quickly helped her up in spite of Nick's glare. Once she was standing, she nearly collapsed again as the weight of what had happened rested fully on her. Tears welled up in her eyes and spilled down her cheeks.

"I don't have $300,000," she groaned. "All my money is tied up in the shop and the cottage." She dabbed at her cheeks roughly with her hand. "I have some stocks and some money in a retirement account, but not nearly enough. There's no way I could get that kind of money."

"Don't worry about that now," Nick insisted. "The full weight of the Orcas Island Sheriff's Department is going to be on this."

"On a dognapping?" Kaylee asked, disbelief dripping from every word.

"On an attack," Nick said. "And when we find the person who attacked our forensic botanist, we'll find Bear."

"And I'll help search for Bear," Reese said. "I bet I won't be the only one either. You have a lot of friends here, Kaylee, and people love Bear, including Nick and me. If you won't go to the hospital, we'll get a ride to the theater and see if everyone there can account for their whereabouts."

Nick shook his head. "If Kaylee won't go to the hospital, you should drive her home."

"Without Bear?" Kaylee hated how close her voice was to a whine. She knew how lost she sounded. She normally prided herself on her ability to deal with whatever came along, but how could she go home when someone was holding her best friend for ransom? Bear was probably afraid—he might even be hurt. She began to shake again.

Nick must have caught on to her grief because he handed a set of keys to Reese. "Take my car and drive to the theater to get yours. You can leave mine at the theater, since I'll need to go question people. Take this one home," he added, gesturing to Kaylee. "She doesn't need to be investigating. I'll handle it."

Kaylee had no interest in being shuffled from one car to another, but she didn't mind not trudging through the rain again. As she walked out of the shed, she held herself as straight as possible, stubbornness and pride being the only things keeping her from collapsing. She felt a tiny twinge of relief when she realized it had stopped raining.

Though her clothes were far from dry, most of the mud on them was dry enough to flake off as she walked with Reese to Nick's off-duty car, a classic red Jeep Wrangler. "I'm not going home," she said when Reese opened the passenger door for her.

Reese offered her a tight smile. "I didn't expect you to. I hope you know Nick will have my head for this. Let's go find out what happened."

The rehearsal was over when they arrived at the theater and entered the auditorium. Members of the cast were dressing to leave. Kaylee tried to watch for which coats were damp, but everyone seemed to be moving too much. *I'm so tired, I'm loopy.*

"Your friends went home, and so should you," Rhett snapped as he stormed toward Reese and Kaylee and shooed them into the lobby. Though he wasn't yet in his overcoat, Kaylee saw he wore a scarf and was pulling on gloves.

With her attention on everyone's clothes, it took Kaylee a moment to process what Rhett had said. She was glad to hear that DeeDee and her family had gone. She couldn't imagine how the girls would respond to news of Bear's abduction.

Rhett eyed Kaylee up and down. "Since it appears that you took a trip through a mud puddle, maybe you should try showering too."

"Rhett!" Belinda appeared at the lobby door, then quickly joined them. She wore a long wool coat and elegant leather gloves. Both dachshunds walked on leashes at her side, so heartbreakingly like Bear. "Don't be rude," Belinda scolded her husband. "Kaylee, what happened? Are you all right?"

From Belinda's horrified expression, Kaylee was glad she hadn't seen herself. "I was walking Bear behind the theater and someone attacked me." Her voice grew choked as she added, "They've . . . they've taken Bear."

Belinda's hand flew to her mouth. "No! We should go out to the shed. Sullivan was in the shed."

"I went there first. There was a note there. The person who has Bear is demanding $300,000."

"Oh dear," Belinda said, her voice weak with horror. "It has to be the same person who took Sullivan. He probably thought Bear was mine. They look identical."

Kaylee hadn't considered that. She stood silently for a moment, working out the possibility. The note hadn't had Bear's name on it. Her gaze drifted to the little dachshunds beside Belinda. They were the exact image of Bear.

"Kaylee!" Quinn trotted up to join the group. "What happened to you?"

"She was attacked. Could you go get her a glass of water, please?" Belinda asked, then she nudged Rhett. "And you go get her a chair. She's clearly about ready to fall down."

Quinn spun and hurried off, but Kaylee spoke up before Rhett could go for a chair. "I'm all right, but I need to know where everyone was when I was attacked."

"You can't be planning to blame this on any of us," Rhett spluttered.

"Stop it, Rhett," Belinda said. "Of course we're to blame. Whoever took Bear must have thought he was one of our dogs." She reached out and took Kaylee's hand, sending flakes of dirt falling from Kaylee's jacket. "Don't you worry about the money. I'll take care of it."

Rhett surprised Kaylee by agreeing. "Of course we'll pay to get your dog back. Bear is a great little guy." The sudden change made Kaylee's aching head spin.

Belinda gave her husband a pleased smile before poking

him gently and saying, "Chair?"

As he strode away, Kaylee said faintly, "I can't ask you to pay Bear's ransom." *Though I have no idea how I'd get the money any other way.*

"Don't be silly. I have more than enough money, and none of this would have happened if I hadn't pulled you and Bear into the theater. I will do whatever I can to get him back for you, as you got my dog back for me. Money doesn't matter. Bear does."

The simplicity of that last statement and the support behind it brought tears to Kaylee's eyes again. "Thank you." She startled when someone tapped her on the shoulder and turned to see Mike Mortenson holding a glass of water. He offered it to her. "Quinn told me to give you this," he said. "I'm glad you're all right."

"I won't be all right until I find Bear," Kaylee said, but she took the glass of water and thanked him for it. She hadn't realized how thirsty she was until the glass was empty.

"Deputy Durham is on his way," Reese said, speaking for the first time as he stepped closer to Kaylee, subtly putting himself between her and Mike. "He's going to want to know where everyone was near the end of the rehearsal."

"We'll answer any questions he has," Belinda said firmly. "I'll go gather the rest of the troupe." She pointed at Mike. "Stay here and make sure Kaylee gets a chair. I'm not sure where Rhett has gone."

"I'll go hunt for him," Reese said, he touched Kaylee's arm. "Will you be okay?"

"I'm fine."

As Reese and Belinda headed into the theater, Kaylee peered around the lobby. There were several chairs against one wall, but Rhett was nowhere to be seen. Why hadn't he brought one of those chairs? Mike trotted over to fetch the closest chair and Kaylee followed him.

"No need to move it," she said. "I can sit there."

He put the chair down. Kaylee noticed that Mike wasn't dressed for the weather outside. Instead he simply wore a blazer over a dark T-shirt, though he was wearing leather gloves.

"Are your hands cold?" she asked.

Mike stared down at his hands and shook his head. "I'm doubling as a stagehand for rehearsals. Pulling ropes was giving me blisters." He pulled off one glove to show Kaylee a blister in the web of his hand.

"Ouch," Kaylee said sympathetically.

Mike shifted on his feet. "I saw you go outside with Bear. I almost offered to walk him for you. I didn't want you to go out in the rain. It's too cold."

"If you were doing the stagehand chores, you'd probably know where everyone was when I went outside with Bear."

He bobbed his head. "Most of the extras were on stage since they were doing the town crowd scenes. Belinda and Rhett were coming on and off, so I can't say exactly where they might have been. Onstage or in the wings, probably. Quinn had been on the stage because she's helping wrangle the kids, but I don't think she was on when you left." Kaylee noticed Mike seemed evasive when he talked about Quinn. *Why was that?* She noticed his tone evened out as he continued rattling off the rest of the people. "That other man, the handyman, he was off in the wings farthest from the backstage door. I know he was over there because Delia complained."

"Where was Delia?" Kaylee asked.

"She's not in the scene," Mike said, "so she was helping with stagehand duties. Well, she was supposed to be, but mostly she was sitting in one of the prop chairs in the wings. Her head still hurts, I think."

"And where was Elliot?" Kaylee asked. "Was he in that scene?"

Mike shook his head. "I think he was in his dressing room. Belinda had talked about doing some late scenes he's not in, so he didn't even need to be here, but he came in anyway. I think he gets lonely. He hangs out here a lot."

Kaylee wondered idly if Elliot Wythe would be able to upend a picnic table onto her. He wasn't a young man, but actors were often in better shape than they seemed at first glance. She was still thinking about it when Nick strode in.

"Kaylee!" the deputy said sharply. "Didn't I tell you to go home? Where's Reese?"

"He went to help find Rhett," Kaylee said. "Rhett disappeared when he was supposed to be getting me a chair." She gestured around the lobby. "Apparently he couldn't find any of the chairs here."

"Interesting." Before Nick could say more, the doors to the audience opened and actors came pouring into the lobby, with Rhett and Belinda taking the lead, and Reese ambling along at the end. "Oh perfect," Nick said. "I have questions for all of you. I'll need to track your movements around the time Miss Bleu was attacked."

"Are you blaming one of us for this?" Rhett demanded. "No one in this troupe would attack a young woman."

"I'm searching for answers, Mr. Case," Nick said. "And the way I find them is to ask questions and gather information."

"And we will cooperate fully," Belinda insisted, giving her husband a sidelong glance. She clapped her hands and surveyed the actors around her. "I expect everyone to help in any way they can. If any of you aren't willing to do whatever is necessary to find Bear, then you might as well hand in your resignation because you won't be part of my troupe."

The actors all bobbed their heads. Kaylee was comforted slightly by Belinda's show of support, but she also saw Rhett bristle at the word "my." She examined the rest of the actors, whose faces all reflected various levels of concern. Of course, they were actors, so there was no telling what was going on behind the facade. There could be a bad guy hidden among the good.

Kaylee finally spoke up. "I was pushed from behind. And I don't know how anyone could have gotten behind me in the little grassy space out back unless that person came from inside the theater."

"There were a lot of people here tonight," Rhett said. "Any of them could have come backstage and gone out the door, which is why we should have had closed rehearsals."

"We could hardly do that," Belinda said wearily. "Some of the actors were children. Still, it's a dark night. Maybe the person was already hiding out there and you didn't see them?"

"That's a possibility," Kaylee said hesitantly. "But I think Bear would have realized it." As she said Bear's name, she had to fight down a sob.

"I checked the logs for the security system," Reese said. "The backstage door opened twice in the time period when Kaylee was out there. The first was her and Bear. The second must have been her attacker."

"Logs?" Rhett repeated harshly. "What are you talking about? You're making things up."

Reese gave the red-faced man a withering stare. "Clearly you don't know how your own security system works." He explained about the logging feature. "The door opened a second time."

Nick spoke up, his voice loud to cut through the murmurs starting in the room. "So it sounds as if someone from inside the theater went out, pushed Kaylee to the ground, and shoved the picnic table over onto her." He pointed his pen at Rhett. "Was it you, Case?"

"It couldn't have been," Belinda insisted before Rhett could say anything. "I'll grant you that my husband is being a bit of a dolt, but he didn't go out the backstage door. He was on the stage with me and a whole bunch of other people."

Belinda's voice rang with perfect sincerity. And it supported what Mike had said. Rhett might be going out of his way to seem like a villain, but he couldn't possibly have attacked Kaylee and taken Bear.

So who had?

18

On Thursday morning, Kaylee woke with a start after a night of fitful sleep. For an instant, she checked the mattress beside her for Bear. When she realized he wasn't there, she burst into tears. Finally, she regained some control and shuffled off to the shower to get ready for work.

When she stepped outside, she shivered against the biting cold blowing in over the water. Did the people who had Bear care enough to keep him warm? Did they care? She blinked quickly before tears could overcome her again and hurried to her car.

As she drove through Turtle Cove, Kaylee noticed that Christmas decorations had crept into window displays. How could she celebrate Thanksgiving or Christmas or anything if she didn't find her little dog? Shaking off that kind of thinking, she slipped into her parking space behind The Flower Patch and strode up to the shop, putting on her best game face.

All her efforts crumbled as soon as Mary greeted her with a hug and a mug of coffee. Kaylee sobbed into Mary's shoulder as her friend murmured quiet reassurances. "Reese called this morning. Finding Bear is a priority for the whole town. We'll get him back, Kaylee." Mary let go of Kaylee and pressed the coffee mug into her hand.

"I just feel so . . . lost without him." Kaylee wrapped her hands around the mug, wishing the warmth could permeate her whole body. She felt as if she'd never be warm again.

"You can stay home if you need to," Mary said gently.

Kaylee shook her head. "Work will help." She waved toward the worktable. "I'm going to get right to our list of orders. I'm not fit company right now."

"That's fine," Mary answered. "Let me know if you need anything. I'll handle the sales floor."

Kaylee blinked against another rush of tears at Mary's sympathy. As she prepared her work space, she considered what she had missed in the last few days. There must have been something for her and Bear to end up in such a horrible situation.

Yeah, hissed a nasty voice in her head. *You didn't butt out when you were warned to.*

Well, kidnapping my dog is a good way to ensure that I'll be sticking my nose in more than ever, she told it.

Kaylee picked up the first order slip and saw that someone wanted a small arrangement that could be preserved by pressing or drying all the flowers. She opened the cooler and sorted through her stock, ticking off the flowers in her head that would preserve well. She had plenty, so she set the vase on the table and began gathering the blooms. *I need to reexamine everything now that we know nothing that has happened has been an accident.* Someone had a hand in everything, from Delia's attack to Rhett's near accident to dognapping both Sullivan and Bear. *What do all those things have in common?*

"Attacking Delia and Rhett could wreck the plan for the theater," Kaylee murmured as she clipped the stems on the first of the daisies for the arrangement. Daisies were lovely and delicate when pressed.

As she contemplated varietals that preserved well, the flowers left at the theater came to mind. "Why would anyone leave lilies?" Kaylee said aloud. "Why flowers at all? Flowers aren't much of a threat."

Or are they? The mystery blooms were *Lilium auratum,* which Kaylee herself associated with funerals. *But that would be a pretty obscure threat, wouldn't it?*

She began slipping flowers into the vase while she pondered the lilies. Maybe obscure was part of the plan. Maybe it was only meant to be understood by one person. Maybe it was a targeted message.

Kaylee clipped more stems and continued contemplating the situation. At the theater, Belinda had clearly thought the lilies were some kind of token of appreciation from a fan, so obviously the message wasn't for her. Rhett had never been happy about them. Granted, Rhett didn't seem to be happy about much, so that wasn't proof of anything. Still, if the flowers were meant to threaten Rhett, it would explain why someone nearly ran him over.

Kaylee sighed. None of that explained why anyone would attack Delia or steal Belinda's dog. She ran her fingers lightly down the stem of a spray of baby's breath. *Gypsophila paniculata*, so common in arrangements. Always in plain sight but so seldom noticed for itself. Was there something in plain sight at the theater that she wasn't noticing?

Kaylee tried thinking of each of the people involved in the Ropeworks Playhouse. Belinda seemed to be the focus of some of the events. The fan note must have been for her, and it was her dog that had been taken the first time. Belinda clearly believed Bear had been mistakenly stolen by the same person, but Kaylee thought that was doubtful. She thrust another sprig of baby's breath into the vase and then picked through the small pile of *Limonium sinuatum*—the purple of the statice would add the pop of color the little arrangement needed, and the flowers kept their color even when dried.

Then again, if Belinda *was* the focus, it might explain running over Rhett. If Belinda had a stalker who was trying to get closer to her by taking her dog and leaving her flowers, the same person might try to remove Rhett from the picture. Kaylee huffed. "That sounds like the plot of a particularly implausible thriller," she said. And it didn't explain why someone left a ransom note for Bear. That suggested the focus was money.

Kaylee's hands shook when she thought about Bear. She was so grateful to Belinda for offering to pay the ransom. It would take Kaylee a long time to repay that much money, but she'd gladly do it. She'd do anything to get her little dog home safe. The flowers in front of her blurred in a new wash of tears. She probably would have fallen apart again if Mary hadn't stuck her head around the doorway just then.

Mary's expression was sympathetic the instant she saw Kaylee's face. "You have a visitor," she said gently. "It's Reese."

Kaylee grabbed a tissue from a nearby box to dab her eyes. She considered going to the bathroom to splash cold water on her face, but she knew she wouldn't be fooling anyone. Reese would know what a wreck she was over Bear, so with a deep breath she straightened her spine and headed into the front part of the shop with as cheerful an expression as she could manage.

Thankfully, Reese pretended not to notice her swollen eyes. "I have some ideas about Bear," he said. "And I thought you might want to go with me."

She shot a questioning glance toward Mary who made a shooing motion. "Go. Anything for Bear."

Gratitude washed over Kaylee again. *I have amazing friends.* "Let's go," she told Reese.

He chuckled, though not with the lightness that usually marked their interactions. "Don't you want to know where I'm whisking you off to?"

"If you think it'll help Bear, that's enough for me."

Kaylee grabbed her coat and purse as Reese explained his thinking. "I believe whoever took Bear is associated with the theater," he said. "Everything points to that place. And that means the person had a very short amount of time to grab Bear before their absence would be noted."

"That makes sense," Kaylee agreed as Reese helped her with her coat.

"And so I'm thinking they couldn't have gone far. Bear may be *at* the theater."

"I'm not so sure," Kaylee said. "He would have been barking his head off. The dognapper would have had to put him someplace where he wouldn't be heard." *Assuming he was alive.* An icy chill slipped up her back as Reese opened the door. She froze, watching him in terror. "Do you think Bear is still alive?"

"I'm certain he is," Reese said firmly. "The person is after money. And whoever it is must know you might insist on proof that Bear's okay."

"Right." Kaylee clung to that, pushing aside her fears for Bear. There was no way she could function if she gave them space in her head.

As they drove to the theater, Kaylee went over the musings she'd had while working on the flowers. "I wonder if Belinda might be the focal point for all of this," she said finally.

"Do you think Belinda knows anything she's not saying?" Reese asked.

"I'm not sure." Kaylee fidgeted with a tassel on her coat, unable to be still when she so desperately needed to be moving, searching for Bear. "She let Rhett talk her into firing Bear from the play, though I don't get the feeling she's very happy with him right now."

"Rhett is an enigma," Reese said.

"He's hiding something. I only wish I knew what it was."

The parking lot at the theater was virtually empty, with only a single, slightly battered old Ford sedan parked close to the building.

"Doesn't appear that there's a rehearsal today," Reese said.

"But someone's here." Kaylee gestured toward the sedan. "Hopefully it's someone who will let us in."

"That's not important." Reese reached into the pocket of his coat and pulled out a key. "Belinda gave me a key when I first agreed to be a part-time handyman. Actually, this works out. If we're going to search, the fewer people around, the better."

"You really think Bear could be in the theater?" Kaylee asked. "Nick searched there."

"He did, but this old building has more than a few secrets," Reese said. He hopped out of the truck and came around to open Kaylee's door. The cold felt more intense than when they'd left the flower shop. Kaylee hoped Bear *was* in the theater. At least he'd be warm.

Reese led her around the rear of the building. "My key is for the stage door."

"Won't we trip the alarm?" Kaylee asked.

Reese shook his head. "There's a short delay to give a chance to disarm the system from the inside. I've got the code."

"The room you were in the other day when I couldn't find you," Kaylee said. "Could Bear be in there?"

"I imagine Nick would have searched there, but we'll check." Reese unlocked the door and hurried inside to get to the keypad mounted on a nearby wall. Kaylee followed him in. Once the security system was disarmed, Reese said, "I have an ace in the hole. You know how I helped with the remodel?"

Kaylee nodded, not really in the mood for beating around the bush.

"I happen to be buddies with the guy who was general contractor for the job. He still has copies of all the plans. And I woke him up at dawn this morning." Reese chuckled. "He actually might be an ex-friend because of that, but he was willing to let me look at the plans once he heard about Bear. He's a dog lover himself."

"Do you have the plans?" Kaylee asked.

Reese shook his head, then produced some thin sheets of paper from his coat. "But I have tracings of some interesting hidey-holes in this building. Places I'm sure Nick wouldn't have known about and wouldn't have searched."

A small bubble of hope expanded in her chest. "Let's get going."

"We can start here." Reese led her to a set of tall cabinets nearby. They opened two different cupboards, both stuffed with spare rope, clamps, and other assorted bits of gear that Kaylee assumed must be useful in a theater. Even without the equipment inside, however, the little cupboards wouldn't have given Bear much room, and he'd have barked or scratched to get out.

As Reese closed the second cupboard, they heard a shout from down the hall. "Hey, what are you guys doing here?" Mike Mortenson called.

"Hunting for Bear," Kaylee explained.

Mike gave her a confused look and scratched his head. "In a cupboard?" He shook his head. "I don't think you two should be in here when Rhett and Belinda are at home."

"I believe Bear is in the theater somewhere," Reese said. He stepped toward the other man, crowding his space slightly. "The time frame last night makes it almost a sure thing. I'm going to find him, and if you get in the way, I'll knock you down."

Mike's jaw tightened, and Kaylee thought he might try to hit Reese. She hurried closer. "Belinda would want you to help find Bear. You know she would."

Mike's gaze focused on Kaylee and immediately softened, though he still didn't seem happy. "I have to call the Cases and tell them you're here. I have to. They're my bosses. But I won't get in your way."

While Mike stepped aside and pulled out his phone, Reese breezed right past him, peering at the blueprint tracings he'd pulled from his coat. Kaylee stayed close behind Reese, and she heard Mike following them.

"This next spot is in the furnace room," Reese said. "There's a cupboard I never noticed, apparently." He gave Kaylee a rueful look. "This isn't the cleanest spot in the theater."

Kaylee nearly rolled her eyes. "You saw me last night. Clean isn't that important right now."

Reese led her to a door she'd never have detected. It was tucked into the shadows and painted to match the wall closely. The door had no handle, only a small indentation to slide it to one side. "A pocket door," Reese explained. "Makes it blend in better."

The room beyond was pitch-black, and Reese had to walk in to pull a string for the light. The space was small, but the low-wattage bulb still left plenty of shadows.

"Wouldn't better lighting help you work in here?" Kaylee asked.

"Low wattage saves money," Mike offered from his spot in the doorway. "And Rhett is all about that."

Reese peered around the room. "Do you know where the cupboard is in here?"

"I wasn't aware there *was* a cupboard in here," Mike said. "I've only seen the ones you just checked. Rhett hasn't asked me to play furnace keeper. Yet. But I'm sure it's coming."

Kaylee walked to the farthest corner of the wall where Reese was hunting. Something had caught her eye, something that gleamed slightly even in the deep shadows. She reached out and touched a small, shiny lock. "Reese," she squeaked. "This is the same kind of lock that was on the shed."

Reese leaned over. "It is. Let's get it off there." He looked around the room, then headed toward a toolbox against the wall.

"What are you doing?" Mike asked while Reese rummaged in the box. "Maybe we should wait until the Cases get here. You don't want to be breaking any of their stuff."

Reese stood up, a hammer in one hand. "Actually I do." He headed over to the lock and began pounding on it.

Kaylee stood behind him, her hand covering her mouth as nausea churned in her stomach. With all the banging, surely Bear would bark if he were in there. *Bark, Bear. Please, bark.*

Though Mike protested the damage a couple more times, Reese paid him no attention at all. He pounded until the lock sprang open and he pulled it free.

Kaylee held her breath as Reese yanked open the cupboard door. The inside of the cupboard was dark, but Kaylee could see well enough.

Inside the small space, a dachshund lay in a heap—deathly still.

19

Kaylee sobbed out Bear's name as she gathered the dog into her arms. The bow tie she'd fastened so neatly before they came to rehearsals hung crookedly below the collar of the rain poncho. She held her ear against his chest and heard his heart beating, slow and steady. "He's alive!"

Reese put an arm around Kaylee as she burst into tears. "It's going to be okay," he said. "We'll take him straight to the vet. I'm calling the sheriff's department right now." He pointed at Mike. "You stay away from that cupboard."

Mike nodded wordlessly, his gaze never moving from Bear's limp body.

Reese made the call, then shucked off his coat and handed it to Kaylee. "Wrap Bear in this. We don't want him to get cold on the way to the truck."

Kaylee wrapped the coat around Bear and, with Reese's arm around both of them to block the wind, they hurried out to the truck. On the whole drive, Kaylee prayed softly under her breath, and Reese drove in silence.

At the vet clinic, Kaylee couldn't stop a sob when she had to hand Bear over.

"We'll take good care of him. I promise," Dr. Melody said gently.

Kaylee bobbed her head, but that was all she could manage.

Reese sat beside Kaylee in the waiting room, and she thought she should say something about how grateful she was for his support, but the effort of talking was simply too monumental, so she stared at the door leading to the rear of the clinic. Bear was back there somewhere, and she could do nothing at all for him but pray. So she did that.

Time passed in a fog. At one point, Reese stepped away to talk to someone on the phone. Kaylee wondered idly if it was Nick, but the curiosity passed as quickly as it came. She didn't care about solving anything. She only wanted Bear to be all right.

She startled when Reese touched her arm. "Sorry," he said. He pressed a paper to-go cup into her hand. "I stopped by Death by Chocolate and got you some coffee. Mary was there too, and she and Jessica send their love."

She hadn't even noticed him leave. "Thank you." She wrapped her hands around the cup, soaking in the warmth, but didn't drink. The door to the inner office opened, and Kaylee jumped to her feet so quickly that a little of the hot coffee sloshed onto her hand. She merely shook it off. "Is he all right?"

Dr. Melody's eyes were kind. "He will be. He's been sedated, and he was a little dehydrated. I think he was kicked at some point and he'll be sore from that, but I did an X-ray and there are no broken bones. We've given him an IV and brought his fluids up, and his vitals are all strong. At this point, I think all we can do is let him sleep it off."

"Can I see him?"

"Sure. But remember, he's not awake. It might be a little unnerving."

"I don't care. I just need to be with him."

Dr. Melody led Kaylee through the door and past all the examining rooms. A few animals lay on soft pet beds in wire crates in the back room. Kaylee spotted Bear immediately and rushed to the enclosure. She opened the door and reached in to stroke her dog's smooth flank.

"You don't need to stay," the vet said. "He's going to sleep all morning. I'd let you take him home, but I think he's better off here until he wakes up. That way we can keep checking his vitals."

"Can I stay with him for a few minutes?" Kaylee asked.

Dr. Melody agreed and left Kaylee alone.

"Who did this to you?" Kaylee whispered to Bear as she continued to pet him. "I'm going to figure this out. No one is going to hurt you again."

Kaylee couldn't have said how long she stood by the cage, gently petting Bear, but she hardly noticed when the door to the recovery room opened and Reese walked in. "Kaylee, I talked to Dr. Melody. She promised to call the second Bear wakes up. Maybe you'd feel better with a little distraction?"

Kaylee continued to stroke Bear. "I'm afraid to leave him. I just got him back, and he's not even awake. I don't know if he's really okay."

"Dr. Melody won't let anyone in to hurt Bear," Reese said. "She said all he needs now is sleep. Maybe we should let him do that."

Kaylee stared at Bear, watching the slow rise and fall of his chest. She hated to leave him, but she didn't want to do anything to make things worse. Finally, she stepped back and closed the door. "I should get to the shop. Mary must be worried."

Reese smiled. "Good plan."

At The Flower Patch, Mary met Kaylee with a hug, bustling her into the shop and over to the stool behind the counter. "How is Bear?" she asked.

"Dr. Melody says he'll be okay. I trust her." Kaylee's voice caught and she couldn't say anything else.

"You just sit," Mary insisted. "I'll get you some tea." Mary turned toward Reese who stood in the doorway still. "Do you want a cup?"

Kaylee felt as if she were moving in slow motion as she followed Mary's gaze.

"I have to go," Reese said, his voice full of apology. "I

promised to check the furnace at the church."

"Thank you," Kaylee told him, "for everything."

"I'm glad Bear's going to be okay." He seemed as if he wanted to say more, but instead he waved and left the shop.

After Reese was gone, Kaylee drifted into the kitchen to wait for tea. While she sipped it, Kaylee had a stern talk with herself. Bear was going to be *fine*. She wouldn't consider any other option, and she wouldn't spend the rest of the morning on edge. She'd accomplish something. "Have we had many customers?"

"Not so far," Mary said. "It's gotten so cold. I don't think we're going to see much foot traffic today."

Kaylee nodded. She didn't mind. "Any new orders?"

"No, but I booked a consultation for a winter wedding. You're meeting the bride and groom next week."

Thank goodness it wouldn't be today. "That sounds good." Kaylee didn't feel up to talking about all the questions surrounding Bear, and Mary was gracious enough to follow her lead. They chatted about wedding flowers until Kaylee finished her tea and felt much more like herself.

Kaylee busied herself with a variety of tasks around the shop and greeted their occasional customers with what she hoped was her normal enthusiasm, but a part of her was always listening for the call from the vet letting her know Bear was awake. She'd passed an hour of fairly distracted shopkeeping when Mike Mortenson came in, bundled up against the cold and carrying a white pastry box with the logo from Death by Chocolate.

Kaylee remembered the stricken way he'd looked at Bear, and hoped the man in front of her wasn't involved in whatever was going on at the theater. He held out the box. "I asked the lady next door what kinds of things you buy for yourself," he said ducking his head shyly. "I wanted to say that I was sorry about getting in your way when you were searching for Bear.

I didn't think he could possibly be at the theater, and I was worried about my job." He peered at her, his expression earnest.

"That's all right," Kaylee said. She couldn't help but be touched. "You didn't have to bring me anything, but that's very kind. Thank you."

Mike's face reddened. "It's nothing. Is your dog going to be okay?"

"The vet says he'll be fine. He was drugged." She hesitated and then added, "Someone from the theater must have put him in that cupboard. Do you know who would do that?"

"No way." Mike leaned toward her, his expression intense. "No one at the theater would hurt a dog."

"But someone did," she said, slipping behind the counter. She felt better with something between her and the overly demonstrative actor.

Mike ran a hand through his hair and paced back and forth in front of the counter. "I have thought and thought about everyone I saw last night." He stopped. "I only noticed one weird thing, and I'm sure it had nothing to do with you or your dog."

"What weird thing?" Kaylee asked.

He shifted and paced, clearly battling with himself, until he finally stopped and shoved his hands into his jacket pockets. "I saw Quinn at the stage door. But this must have been before you went out because I'd seen you backstage."

Quinn? Kaylee couldn't imagine the pleasant young woman having anything to do with drugging Bear or attacking Kaylee. "Maybe she simply wanted some air."

He shook his head. "She let someone in. A guy. He was probably a few years older than her, but not much. And he was shifty-looking, I thought. Quinn let him in, but she didn't seem happy about it."

"What happened after he came in?" Kaylee asked.

Mike shrugged. "He kissed her cheek, but she didn't appear to appreciate that. I was going to find out if she was okay, but she grabbed the sleeve of the guy's coat and hauled him toward the dressing rooms. I figured it was her business."

"Why didn't you tell anyone about this guy last night?" Kaylee asked.

"Quinn is my boss's niece. I thought the Cases would want to hear about it before I blabbed it around. And I like Quinn. I was going to tell her that I saw her and see what she said. But then I saw Bear this morning." He shook his head. "I don't think Quinn would do that, but I don't know who the guy was. Or what he might do."

"Did you see the guy again?" Kaylee asked.

"No, but that's not surprising. I was busy." He huffed. "I wish Rhett would let us bring in the real stage crew. That guy is so cheap lately."

Kaylee had found the information about Quinn interesting, but she knew something strange was happening with Rhett, so she decided to nudge Mike a little. "Did you notice Rhett missing at any point during the rehearsal time? Especially near the end?"

"I didn't notice. I was trying to do the work of a whole team. I'm sorry."

The door opened then, and Kaylee was surprised to see two dachshunds scramble in. For an instant, she thought one might be Bear, but then realized how silly that was when Belinda walked in, holding the dogs' leashes. "I heard you found Bear at the theater," the actress said without preamble. "Is he all right?"

"The vet says he will be," Kaylee replied. "He was drugged."

Belinda's face paled. "I can't tell you how bad I feel. I'm sure someone mistook Bear for Sullivan or Gilbert. Why is someone after the dogs? They haven't hurt anyone ever!" She handed the leashes to Mike without a word and set her purse on the counter to pull out her wallet. "I'll pay the vet's fees."

"That's not necessary." Kaylee put a hand on Belinda's. "I'm grateful that you would have paid the ransom, but we can't be sure whether Bear could have been the target all along. We do know that he was stashed at the theater. Do you have any idea who might have done this?"

Belinda blinked at her. "None of us, of course." She addressed her next comment to Mike. "Do you think anyone in the troupe is capable of this?"

Mike shook his head. "But we're all actors. In a way, we lie for a living. I'm not sure I truly know anyone there." He handed Belinda the leashes. "And speaking of making a living, I need to get to the theater. Your husband left me a long list of jobs for today." He nodded to Kaylee and left the shop.

Mike's comment about lying set off something in Kaylee's brain. She waited until the door closed behind Mike, then tentatively broached the subject of Rhett's alibi. "You said Rhett was with you when I was attacked last night. But he wasn't, was he?"

Belinda had been watching the door as well, but her attention refocused on Kaylee. "I would hardly have said he was if he wasn't."

"You might. He's your husband. You love him. And you told me he's been acting oddly."

"He was with me," Belinda said, seemingly ready to stand her ground, but then she crumbled and finished, "some of the time." She placed her hands on the counter and leaned toward Kaylee, her gaze earnest. "Rhett wouldn't hurt anyone, and he certainly wouldn't hurt Bear. He's not like that, and he *loves* dogs."

Kaylee didn't argue with her, but she knew she needed to talk to Nick about Rhett. Then she considered Belinda carefully, weighing whether to bring up Quinn. Was Belinda aware of her niece's secret meeting? But before Kaylee could speak, the phone interrupted them.

All thoughts of questioning Belinda flew out of Kaylee's head as she grabbed the phone. "Hello?"

"Kaylee?" The veterinarian's warm voice was full of cheer. "Someone is awake. And I think he's eager to see you."

20

When Kaylee arrived at the veterinary clinic, she was surprised to find Nick in the waiting room. Before she could ask why he was there, he gave her a quick hug. "I'm so glad to hear Bear is okay," he said. "Dr. Melody told me he woke up."

"Yes, I can't wait to see him." She checked in with the receptionist, who disappeared into the back room. Kaylee turned back to her friend. "What brings you here?"

"Evidence collection," Nick answered. "Dr. Melody combed Bear's coat, so I'll be taking that evidence, but she also found a surprise when they were examining him."

"A surprise?" Kaylee echoed. "I didn't hear about this."

"I imagine she thought you'd want to focus on his health. Apparently Bear bit someone. Dr. Melody said there was skin caught in his teeth, which is a big break for us. Once we run some tests and figure out who Bear bit, we'll find who took him."

"Do you think he bit someone's hand?"

"That does seem the most likely spot," Nick said.

Kaylee thought of the people she'd seen at the theater after Bear was taken. Most of the actors had been wearing gloves since they were preparing to go out in the cold. And when she'd seen them today, Belinda and Mike had both been wearing gloves. Somehow she couldn't imagine Belinda being involved in a dognapping, not with the way she felt about her own dogs. Mike had shown her the blister on one of his hands, but could he have a bite mark on the other? "Maybe you should have everyone involved show you their hands."

"I was thinking that would be a good first step." Nick crossed his arms over his chest. "My prime suspect is the mystery guy who threatened you behind your shop, and he doesn't work for the theater. At least not openly. I'm concerned that he might flee the island if he hears we found Bear."

"Whoever did it might flee," Kaylee said. She went on to tell Nick what Mike had told her about Quinn. "I wonder if the guy Mike saw might be Quinn's ex. From what I've heard of that guy, he could be comfortable attacking someone or stealing a dog. Maybe the dognapping is separate from the scarred stranger?"

Nick had been taking notes as Kaylee spoke, and he now shut his notebook. "Quinn's mystery visitor is another person to check on. We've had the ferry watched, along with charter and rental boats. If any of the theater folk show up at any of those places, we'll be having a chat."

"With this weather, it's not uncommon for people to wear gloves," Kaylee said. "You won't be able to spot a bite if the culprit is someone we haven't seen."

"That's why we're checking people at the ferry," Nick said. "Including asking to see under gloves."

Kaylee pressed her lips together and glanced toward the door to the recovery area. Why hadn't anyone brought Bear out yet? She forced her attention back to Nick. "If the guy who attacked me was the same one who threatened me, how did he get into the theater?"

Nick snorted. "The theater has been a veritable Grand Central Station. After all, Reese didn't have any trouble getting in."

"Reese had a key."

"Yeah, and I wonder who else has one."

Before Kaylee could respond to that, the door finally opened and Dr. Melody walked out with Bear in her arms and the receptionist close behind. When the dog saw Kaylee, he barked and wagged his tail, though Kaylee noticed the motion was slower than usual.

She hurried across the room and took him in her arms. It was all she could do not to break down again. Her little guy really was okay. "Oh, Bear. My sweet boy," she whispered.

"He'll be moving a little slow as the rest of the sedative leaves his system," Dr. Melody explained. "Give him plenty of fluids and keep him warm. And let me know if he doesn't act completely normal by nightfall."

"I will." Kaylee said as she gave Bear a gentle hug. He nestled close to her, tucking his head under her chin. "Thank you so much, Dr. Melody."

"It's my pleasure. Take care."

After she'd settled the bill, Kaylee carried Bear to Nick. "When you're talking to people today, I'd look harder at Rhett and Belinda. I'm sure she was lying about his being with her last night, and he's been acting very strangely."

"We'll check him out," Nick promised, "along with everyone else. But I'm still sure we're going to find out that mystery man who threatened you is the real culprit. I believe he has some kind of obsession with Belinda. I'm betting he would have insisted on Belinda delivering the dognapping ransom money and grabbed her." He pointed at Kaylee with his notebook. "Mark my words, when we find him, we'll solve everything."

Kaylee didn't argue the point, but she worried that Nick wasn't taking Rhett seriously as a possible suspect. The obsessed-fan theory was compelling, but something about it didn't feel right.

Once she had Bear in the car, she drummed her fingers on the wheel. Before she'd left The Flower Patch, Mary had told Kaylee not to hurry back. Kaylee knew her friend probably meant Kaylee could take Bear home to recover, but with the little dog safely in the car, Kaylee couldn't let go of her desire to find out what had really happened. Besides, Bear wasn't truly safe until the dognapper was caught.

"We need to know," Kaylee said. "*I* need to know." So she pulled out of the parking lot and headed for Robin's Nest. When she arrived, she dressed Bear in the sweater she kept for him in the SUV and scooped him up. "Let's go visit Sullivan and Gilbert."

Bear didn't give his usual answering bark, instead snuggling against her. She almost gave up the idea and took him home where he could rest, but no. It was time to get to the bottom of this.

When she rang the doorbell at the cottage, she could hear Gilbert and Sullivan barking inside. Bear rallied a bit at the sound and gave a single yip in reply. Since the dogs were clearly in the cottage, Kaylee expected Belinda to open the door quickly, but she didn't. Bear wriggled in Kaylee's arms, clearly eager to get in and greet his friends.

Kaylee was heartened to see Bear acting more like himself. "We'll go around to the backyard," she told him. "Maybe Belinda is outside for some reason." She set Bear down, and he immediately began tugging at the leash.

When she reached the back of the cottage, she came to a set of French doors that led out to a patio. Through the doors, she caught sight of a scene inside that made her gasp—the scarred man who had threatened Kaylee was standing opposite Rhett, poking him hard in the chest with one finger. Rhett wasn't resisting at all.

Kaylee decided her best course of action was to return to her SUV and call Nick from there, but before she could retreat, Gilbert and Sullivan scurried to the glass doors, barking wildly. Bear responded in kind.

"No, Bear," Kaylee hissed. She bent to grab him so she could run out of the yard, but one of the French doors flew open and the stranger stood there. A gun was in his hand.

"You come inside," he growled at Kaylee. Bear growled right back. "And bring the mutt."

Kaylee didn't have any choice—she could hardly outrun a bullet—so she followed directions. In the great room of the cottage, Rhett sat in a chair, his head in his hands. Even from where Kaylee stood, she could see the bandage on Rhett's hand. Nearby, Belinda was perched on the edge of a table, her face pale.

"Now that we're all here," the stranger said, turning the gun on Rhett, "I want the money now. And someone better fork it over before I start making people bleed."

"I don't have that kind of cash here," Belinda said. "I can give you what's in the safe, but you're going to have to let me go to the bank for the rest." She shot a withering glare at Rhett. "This never needed to get this bad. I can pay."

"And you will," the scarred man snarled.

"I'm so sorry, Belinda," Rhett said weakly.

"You should be," she snapped. "People have been hurt. Innocent people."

"And more are going to be if you don't follow orders," the stranger said. "Now get me the money."

Belinda stood and lifted her chin. "There's no need to be nasty. The safe is in the bedroom."

"Get to it. Leave the door open so I can see you, and don't try anything cute," the man commanded.

Belinda didn't respond, but she walked through a nearby door, leaving it ajar in her wake. Kaylee saw the stranger's attention was strictly on Belinda so she whispered to Rhett, "What's going on?"

Rhett looked up at her with red, puffy eyes. He'd been crying. "I owe a lot of money to bad people." He swallowed hard. "Gambling. That guy was sent by the people I owe."

The gunman glared at Rhett. "You could have taken care of all this without so much trouble. You knew we wouldn't forget about your debt."

"You left the lilies," Kaylee said. "Didn't you?"

The man appeared pleased, though the expression did nothing to make him seem friendlier. "I'm thinking of adopting that as my calling card. Death flowers." He laughed, a cold sound that made Bear growl. The stranger narrowed his eyes as he glared at Bear, then back at Rhett. "I even snatched your wife's dog to show you how easily I could take something you loved. But you had to go and make me do *this*."

"I didn't have the money," Rhett whispered.

"But she did!" the gunman roared, eliciting a flurry of angry barks from all the dogs.

"I couldn't tell her I was gambling again," Rhett said. "That was the one thing she insisted on before she'd marry me. It's the one thing I knew she'd leave me over. But I was going to get you the money."

Kaylee pointed at the bandage on Rhett's hand. "That's why you took Bear. To pay your debt. You were going to pass off my dog as one of yours because you knew your wife would offer to pay the ransom. And if she didn't—well at least one of your dogs wasn't in danger."

Rhett hung his head.

"And I'll never forgive you for it," Belinda said coldly as she walked into the room, carrying a thick wad of money. "Kaylee is my friend. And even if she wasn't, the fact that you wanted to give up an innocent dog to save your own skin is repulsive." She thrust the cash at the gunman. "I only have ten grand here. You'll have to let me get the rest from the bank."

"I'm sorry," Rhett wailed. "I love you."

Belinda glared at him again. "But not enough to tell me the

truth. And not as much as you love gambling."

"But how could you be in two places at one time?" Kaylee asked. "Bear ran after someone in the dark, but I was pushed from behind."

"Your mutt ran after me," the gunman said. "I gave him a good kick in the ribs."

Kaylee gritted her teeth. Even with the gun in the man's hand, it was all she could do not to rush at him, claws bared, for hurting Bear.

"I was afraid you'd see him." Rhett tilted his head toward the gunman. "I knocked you down. Then when I saw Bear lying where he'd landed after the kick, I saw a way to get the money. So I took him."

"How did you sedate him?" Kaylee demanded, even though she wasn't sure she wanted details.

"A sleeping pill in chicken broth," Rhett said. "He drank it up. He's a trusting dog."

"Enough talk!" the gunman shouted. "Your wife and I have to get to the bank. And that means I have to tie you two up." He swung the gun between Kaylee and Rhett. "Once I have the money, I'll let her go, and she can come here and untie you."

Kaylee doubted the man was going to simply leave so many witnesses alive and well, but she didn't know what she could possibly do about it.

Suddenly all three dachshunds raced toward the front door, barking furiously.

"What the—?" the gunman demanded, turning toward the commotion, his back to Kaylee.

She spotted the heavy metal horse sculpture on a nearby table and grabbed it. She swung it hard and it made contact against the man's upper back and neck, sending him sprawling. The gun flew out of his hand.

Kaylee went after it, but someone beat her to it—Deputy Nick Durham. He scooped up the weapon and put a foot on the gunman's back. "It's okay, Kaylee," he said as he fished his cuffs out. "I've got this one."

Deputy Robyn Garcia quickly joined them and cuffed Rhett. "It was his skin Dr. Melody found," she explained to Kaylee.

"How did you know to come here?" Kaylee asked.

"Somebody hit a panic button that called us," Nick said.

"Yes," Belinda added with no small amount of satisfaction. "I had one installed in the safe. My parents always taught me that you can never be too careful."

"I was already on my way over here with Deputy Garcia to talk to the Cases about everything that's been happening at the theater," Nick said. "So I took the call. Snuck around to peek through the doors to the backyard. When I saw what was going on, I sent Robyn to ring the doorbell, and I took advantage of the distraction." He grinned. "Well, after Kaylee took advantage of it first."

Kaylee winced. "I would gladly have left it for you if I'd known you were coming." She gestured toward Rhett, who sat miserably in handcuffs. "What happens to him?"

"He assaulted you, abducted a dog, and interfered in a police investigation," Nick said. "He's going to jail. It won't be as long a sentence as the mob enforcer here, but he's still in big trouble. Unless he makes some kind of deal to bring in the people he owes all that money to, but that's probably up to the FBI."

"I don't think Belinda had anything to do with any of this," Kaylee said.

"No," Nick agreed. "I don't think she did either."

Belinda sent Kaylee a grateful smile.

When she was eventually allowed to go home, Kaylee was overwhelmed with relief that she and Bear could finally feel safe there. Although she'd never questioned Bear's bravery, it'd be just fine with her if his courage wasn't put to the test again anytime soon—or ever again.

Over the next few days, bits and pieces of information trickled in to fill the rest of the gaps. Although the scarred man had dognapped Sullivan, the strange note found in the dachshund's backpack had actually been from Rhett to Belinda. He'd meant it as a romantic gesture, but had been afraid to admit it was from him when the dog was found. He hadn't wanted the police to find a reason to check into him.

Delia had recanted her recollection of being pushed because she'd received a threatening text from the enforcer, just as Kaylee had. Not wanting to be attacked again, she had told Nick she no longer remembered the incident clearly.

The stranger that Quinn let into the theater on the night Kaylee was attacked had been her ex-boyfriend, which she admitted when asked. "He came all the way out to the island to try to win me back," she told Kaylee. "I guess I felt I owed it to him to hear what he had to say, so I saw him a couple times. I kept it secret so my aunt wouldn't freak." She rolled her eyes. "Jason's apology was the same lame line. I won't be seeing him again. I'm young enough that I have a lot I want to do, but too old to waste my time with someone like that."

With Rhett in jail, Kaylee worried the theater would be shuttered before it ever fully opened, but Belinda was serious about her commitment to the show. She brought the stagehands from the mainland, and Mike took over Rhett's role in the play.

On opening night, Kaylee led Bear into the theater. He

wore a royal blue bow tie, which matched her dress perfectly. The theater lobby was nearly packed, as residents from all over Orcas Island greeted one another before heading in to find their seats. Kaylee was delighted by the crowd and remembered Belinda's dream of turning the Ropeworks Playhouse into the Broadway of the Pacific Northwest. *She might be on her way after all.*

Kaylee startled slightly as someone slipped an arm through hers. "Can you believe we made it?" DeeDee asked.

"How are the girls?"

DeeDee grinned. "Walking on air. You ready to go in?"

"In a minute," Kaylee said. "Reese asked me to wait for him in the lobby. He probably wants to tell me something about the furnace at the cottage. He came over to check it out yesterday."

DeeDee tipped her a sly wink. "I'm sure that's exactly what he wants."

Kaylee gave her a reproving frown for the matchmaking foolishness, but she didn't bother saying anything since DeeDee was giggling. "I'll see you later," her friend said before hurrying over to join Andy.

When Reese finally came through the theater doors, Kaylee almost gasped. He definitely cleaned up well and the dark suit he wore made the most of his tall, muscular build. He caught sight of her and Bear and grinned. As he reached them, he held up his ticket. "Surprise," he said. "When I called Belinda for a ticket, I asked to be seated near you and Bear. This play is best seen with close friends."

Bear gave a single yip of approval and Kaylee took Reese's proffered arm. "I agree," she said. "And since we're so close, I can tell you the truth. I'm glad to be watching from the audience and not the stage, even the wings. I think Bear's theater days are over. I never want to go through that again."

Reese chuckled. "Never say never, Kaylee Bleu. Life is full of surprises."

Kaylee smiled in response. That was one sentiment she couldn't argue with a single bit.

Learn more about Annie's fiction books at

AnniesFiction.com

We've designed the Annie's Fiction website especially for you!

Access your e-books • Read sample chapters • Manage your account

Choose from one of these great series:

Amish Inn Mysteries	Chocolate Shoppe Mysteries
Annie's Attic Mysteries	Creative Woman Mysteries
Annie's Mysteries Unraveled	Hearts of Amish Country
Annie's Quilted Mysteries	Inn at Magnolia Harbor
Annie's Secrets of the Quilt	Secrets of the Castleton Manor Library
Antique Shop Mysteries	Victorian Mansion Flower Shop Mysteries

What are you waiting for? Visit us now at **AnniesFiction.com!**

Don't miss the Secrets of the Castleton Manor Library!

Join Faith Newberry and her cat, Watson, in the quaint town of Lighthouse Bay on Cape Cod in Massachusetts as she marries her love of books to a penchant for sleuthing. After landing her dream job as librarian at Castleton Manor, an upscale literary retreat, Faith is forced to read between the lines and solve the mysteries she finds among the stacks. Faith, Watson, and the lively members of the Candle House Book Club set out to unravel whodunits that might have stumped even Sherlock Holmes. Enjoy the thrill of the hunt with Faith and her friends as they solve puzzling crimes, discover dark secrets, and embrace heartwarming truths that have long been hidden in the voluminous pages of the Castleton Manor Library.

Learn more at AnniesFiction.com!

Treat yourself to the delightful decadence of the **Chocolate Shoppe Mysteries**—stories that are sure to keep you on the edge of your seat!

Follow the clues with Jillian Green in the enchanting town of Moss Hollow, Georgia, as she mixes up a batch of mystery and intrigue. After twenty years away, a career detour, and a large helping of heartbreak, she returns to the land of sweet tea and Southern charm to help her grandmother run the family business, The Chocolate Shoppe Bakery. Along the way, Jillian is surprised to find that what she lacks in culinary skill, she more than makes up for in amateur detective work! Jillian and her sweet new friends in the local baking club embark on investigations into the curious events taking place in their hometown, with reminders all the while that family, friendships—and a dash of adventure—are essential ingredients to a full and happy life.

Find out more at AnniesFiction.com!